ABOUT THE AUTHORS

Bob McCulloch, FCMC, helps senior managers and executives strengthen their creativity and strategic thinking. Over the past 30 years, he has worked with executive teams in virtually every industry sector. Prior to launching his own firm, CYOR Inc., he held strategic positions with IBM Canada, the DMR Group, and Johnston Smith International. He lives in Toronto.

Julia Gluck, FCMC, assists clients in implementing change through the use of continuous workplace learning. She has developed her expertise with firms such as DMR Consulting, Johnston Smith International, and Deltak Inc., and now focuses on teaching. She lives in Toronto.

ABOUT THE ENERGY EXCHANGE™

The **Energy Exchange**™ embraces a set of practices that *liberate* and *direct* the flow of personal creative energy both *within* and *between* people. These practices are embodied in two conceptual models.

The **Vowels of Personal Power** model helps individuals maximize the power of their interactions with others—in a way that is not selfish or manipulative and that strengthens both the *relationship* and the *result* of the interaction.

The **Pentacle Path** lays out a six-part approach to problem solving that helps people generate the best possible solution to a problem or opportunity given the time and resources available. It takes its name from the geometric symbol signifying "vigor" and "wholeness."

The **Energy Exchange**™ is a trademark of CYOR Inc., Toronto, Canada.

How to reach us:
    Bob@TheEnergyExchange.com
    Julia@TheEnergyExchange.com

The Vowels of Personal Power

5 + 1 Ways
to Liberate
Your Creative Energy

Bob McCulloch
Julia Gluck

**BASTIAN
BOOKS**

An Energy Exchange Book
www.TheEnergyExchange.com

BASTIAN BOOKS
A division of Bastian Publishing Services Ltd.
www.bastianpubserv.com

Distributed by Publishers Group Canada
www.pgcbooks.ca

ISBN 0-9780554-3-8

Cataloguing in Publication Data
available from Library and Archives Canada

Editorial: Donald G. Bastian, Bastian Publishing Services Ltd.
www.bastianpubserv.com

Cover design: Daniel Crack
Interior design: Tannice Goddard
Production: Mary Bowness

Printed and bound in Canada by Webcom

Bob:
To the readers of this book who use the practices of
The Energy Exchange to make a difference in this world

Julia:
To those who use their energy to
repair the world one small step at a time

Ask yourself—and yourself alone—one question:
"Does this path have heart?" If it does, the path is good;
if it doesn't, it is of no use.

— DON JUAN, A YAQUI WARRIOR

in *The Teachings of Don Juan*, Carlos Castaneda

Contents

U • Understanding

Preface

Each of us has more than 25 years of experience in management, facilitation, consulting, coaching, and training. We have worked in-house in several organizations and as consultants performing services for many others. During those years, and in our work today, we have observed how some people are marked by a high level of energy, at work and at play, in meetings and in one-on-one conversations. These people seem to make decisions easily, and to have a lighter step in the world. They seem happier and less argumentative. They seem open to people and their ideas, accepting them without judgment or censure. These are the people of whom others say, "They always have good rhythm" or "Everything seems to fall into place for them" or "They always seem to be in the right place at the right time."

We have also observed people whose energy seems to be blocked, both within themselves and in their relationships. Relating to them saps our energy because of the force field they create around themselves filled with politics, rivalry, personality clashes, and their sadness and frustration. Their lives seem to be a chore, leaving them, and those around them, with no time or energy for creative cooperation or personal enjoyment.

We've seen these types of people both in the workplace and in "civilian life"—our families, the community, wherever we go in this world of ours. However, if there's one major point of consensus forming up in our society at the beginning of this century, it is that there is no real distinction between "professional life" and "personal life": everything is personal. Accordingly, what we have observed about personal and interpersonal energy applies equally to life at home and in society and on the job.

That said, it is often worthwhile to make distinctions between different spheres of life when considering the application of theories and methods. That's why this book is about the vowels of personal power and our next book will be about the vowels of professional power. Like this book, the next one will have examples from both arenas. This book addresses personal life in the family, home, and community, and the next will focus on personal life at the professional level.

The backdrop to both books is our theory of what we call an energy exchange in relationships—and our formation of a network of people under the banner of The Energy Exchange, an evolving body of knowledge based on both observation and anecdotal research. Individually and within this network, we have investigated what blocks and unblocks the flow of energy within and between people. We have spent several years testing this framework with individuals in various spheres of life. This book pulls together our theory, practice, and examples to help you and the significant others in your life liberate the creative energies you were born with. We know you will be surprised and delighted with the results.

〜

Speaking of creative energy, we could not have written this book if these people had not made many important contributions in that department:

Charlie Palmgren, who introduced us to Creative InterChange (www.innovativeinterchange.com), and Jim Gaul, who introduced us to Charlie.

Cindy and Timothy Barlow, Mike Flynn, Jake McArthur, and Rod McCulloch, who encouraged us to create this model in the first place.

Dorothy and Rome McCulloch, who edited and advised with respect to the model.

Ted and Jess Overton, who provided many opportunities for creative exchanges of energy.

Our business and personal colleagues who have reviewed the descriptions of the individual practices and given us valuable feedback on their clarity and usefulness.

The many clients who tested the model with us in various forms.

Neighbor and client Jim Heaton, who continually encouraged us and supported our efforts.

Diana Bishop, who led us through an exhaustive investigation of the practices to make them clear and coherent.

Don Bastian, whose optimism, patience, and understanding demonstrated how the energy exchange works to enhance creativity and productivity.

Introduction

Remember the drill?

"Class, please list all the vowels," your teacher would say.

"A, E, I, O, U, and sometimes Y," you and your classmates would respond.

In this book we are building on this age-old mnemonic device, presenting what we call the 5 + 1 vowels of personal power. They are:

- Awareness
- Engagement
- Integrity
- Openness
- Understanding

And as for the "sometimes Y," we discuss it in the conclusion, entitled, with some poetic license, "And Always Why." Why "why"? Because for all of us, our philosophy of life is both the foundation and the result of how we interact with the issues of our lives and the people in our lives.

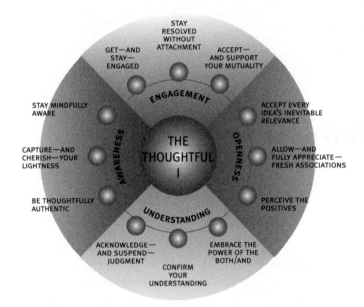

In this book, we take the vowels—A, E, O, and U—and describe three practices of each that will help you achieve mastery of awareness, engagement, openness, and understanding. I, meanwhile, has a chapter of its own and is front and center throughout this book as it works to coordinate and integrate all of the practices.

The 12 practices will enable you, step by step, to access more effective, more powerful, and more creatively energetic ways of relating. They will enable you to liberate your creative energy and transform your relationships. They will enable you to reconnect with your innate ability to create. They will improve your physical, mental, emotional, and even spiritual well-being.

Using these practices is not magical—the process is not one of hocus-pocus but of experimentation, discipline, and constant vigilance. The *results*, however, *are* magical. Once you apply the practices to yourself and then put them to work in a relationship, you will be well equipped to apply them to other relationships, until the patterns, and wonderful relationships, become a natural part of your life. "Things go better with Coke" was one of Coca-Cola's famous taglines. The tagline or constant theme of our work and this book is: *As energy flows, the better life goes.*

The Energy Exchange

Reality conspires against our individual and shared energy. This starts early in our lives, soon after we exit the womb. When children are born, were they able to speak, they would probably say, "I'm in shock. I'm coming out of a warm, wet tank and now it's dry and uncomfortable."

(Bob) My daughter, Rome, was born by caesarian section. I remember her coming out feet first like a big corkscrew. She appeared to be a small, blue Shar-Pei dog with a huge mass of red hair. Within five minutes, the blue was gone, and a bunch of the Shar-Pei folds were gone. I could see through Rome's crying the beginnings of her attempts to become engaged with her environment.

I was fortunate to be able to take parental leave from my management-consulting firm for three months and watch Rome's rapid progression. Day by day she became increasingly **aware** of and **engaged** with her environment. She was totally **open** to life around her and was continually seeking to **understand**—learning, for example, that certain cries prompted certain responses.

> After returning to work, I continued spending lots of time observing her and playing with her. Rome was clearly open to everything. And then, beginning at about 15 months and continuing through her early years, the shoulds and shouldn'ts began to settle in. My wife, Dorothy, and I tried to stay as open as possible, yet the structures continued to form. By the time she was four, it seemed to us that she had developed a set of rules.

The premise of The Energy Exchange, and of this book, is that, like Rome, we are all born bundles of creative energy. When we are little, we live in the present moment. Our memory of the past is short and we have no sense of the future. Everything is now. In our natural state, energy flows freely within us, between us, and in our environment. We're born with the capacity for **awareness, engagement, openness,** and **understanding.**

However, as we develop our own understanding of the world, we extend our list of shoulds and shouldn'ts, works and not-works, "goods" and "bads." The things that work for us become our laws and the things that don't become our taboos. Together these form the basis of our beliefs, many of which become *limiting* beliefs. We begin to apply our past judgments easily and instinctively to current situations, and a lot of what we do becomes automatic.

Soon we begin to live in the past and in the future, failing to leverage the real power of life: the present. Most of us have heard the child's lament, "I can't wait until my next birthday!" With external and internal forces working to obstruct our natural energy, it's not surprising that it's a challenge to remain aware, engaged, and open, continually seeking to understand.

That's where our conscious mind comes in—what we will introduce as our Thoughtful I—which we use to reconnect with our native talents and actively manage our awareness, engagement, openness, and continued quest for understanding.

5 + 1 Ways to Liberate Your Creative Energy

The practices associated with each of the vowels of power in this book will help you liberate your creative energy. Let's take a quick look ahead at the 5 + 1 sections of the book.

I is for Integrity and the Thoughtful I

The Thoughtful I—our conscious thought— *integrates* all the other practices in the vowels of personal power. It intervenes between emotion and response, stays engaged and aware, keeps us positive and open, and helps us take effective action through richer understanding.

A is for Awareness

As we become more *aware* of ourselves and those around us, we learn to handle difficult situations and communicate our feelings with authenticity and tact. We can prevent ourselves from falling victim to overwhelming and negative feelings.

The AWARENESS section of the book explores these three practices:

- Stay Mindfully Aware
- Capture—and Cherish—Your Lightness
- Be Thoughtfully Authentic

E is for Engagement

Once we become more aware of what's happening inside and around us, we learn to stay *personally engaged* with ourselves, in our relationships, and as we move toward our goals.

The ENGAGEMENT section of the book deals with these three practices:

- Get—and Stay—Engaged
- Stay Resolved Without Attachment
- Accept and Support Your Mutuality

O is for Openness

As we move toward greater *openness*, our Thoughtful I begins to see exciting new possibilities. We learn to embrace and accept all the new ideas and possibilities that come our way.

The OPENNESS section of the book describes these three practices:

- Accept Every Idea's Inevitable Relevance
- Allow—and Fully Appreciate—Fresh Associations
- Perceive the Positives

U is for Understanding

The more we *understand*—not just *know about*—a situation, the better we can frame our responses and the better we can take appropriate action. The Thoughtful I and understanding will help us get to a point where we develop a more complete understanding that is physically, mentally, emotionally, and spiritually nuanced.

The UNDERSTANDING section of the book presents these three practices:

- Acknowledge—and Suspend—Judgment
- Confirm Your Understanding
- Embrace the Power of the Both/And

And so … let the journey begin.

INTEGRITY

The journey begins as you activate your Thoughtful I.

As an infant, your *awareness, engagement, openness,* as well as your continual search for *understanding,* were all naturally present. You did not have to consciously manage them because there was nothing standing in their way—no guiding or limiting memories, no established beliefs, no embedded fears.

As an adult, you have lots of things standing in the way of the flow of your personal creative energy, all anchored in your thoughts and beliefs about the way the world works. So to get out of the rut of automatic thoughts, you need to mobilize your conscious thinking—your Thoughtful I.

Your Thoughtful I not only allows you to activate your awareness, engagement, openness, and understanding. It also brings them all together, selecting which practices need to come to the fore at any one time, and putting them into a sequence to generate the greatest positive impact.

So let's look at how your Thoughtful I is uniquely positioned to perform its integrating role.

1

The Thoughtful I

Living with energy and power doesn't happen by chance. It happens through thoughtfulness. Thoughtful people become aware of, engaged in, and open to their environments, while understanding that they don't control them. They influence their environments to help themselves get what they need to get. They recognize that as they put more thought into their lives, they will be more easily able to influence what happens to them.

>   *(Bob)* Ten years ago I changed the name of a company I had started years earlier to CYOR—Create Your Own Reality. My thinking went something like this: Since we're creating our own reality anyway, wouldn't it be more useful to create the reality we want rather than the one that's just happening to us? The implication became very clear to me: If we're going to enrich our lives, have more joyous, powerful, and fun lives, and be more "successful"—however we define the term—we need to be fully engaged. We need to stay aware of what's going on

> within and around us. We need to continuously seek to understand and stay open to all ideas that present themselves.
>
> This requires an enormous amount of thoughtfulness.

It's About I

We believe (and please forgive our grammar) that *life is not about me, it's about I.*

When the focus is on *me,* the energy turns inward. With nowhere to go, the energy becomes blocked, and our view is limited.

When the focus is on *I,* the energy flows. Our view of life becomes wider. Our stance is: How do I get engaged in my environment and start attracting the things to me that I want in my life?

And when we get into a dialogue, whether with a business colleague, a spouse, a child, or a sibling, it is not about me, or what I can get over the other person, or even, at a higher level, what I can get for the good of someone else. It's about how I, in the context of our relationship, can achieve what I want to achieve and how you can achieve what you want to achieve.

When our focus is on "me," we're turned inward and our energy is blocked. When our focus is on "I," we get engaged in our environment and actively work to get what we want in our lives.

By the way, this personal creative energy is always there. Through what we do, we can let it flow easily or let it get blocked. When we get involved with other people, this easy-flowing energy spills over to create a relationship that enables us individually and in relationships to get what all of us want. The four instruments of the Thoughtful I—awareness, engagement, openness, and understanding—help us ground ourselves in the present moment, focusing our energy on getting the most from our lives, and in the process helping others get the most from their lives.

And it's also about "here and now." The power of the Thoughtful I is rooted firmly in the present. The present is the point of power.

We do not control the future; we influence it, and only by what we choose to do now, in this very moment. In this moment of "now," our view of the future and its opportunities and obstacles changes the possibilities. And while we cannot change the facts of the past, our present view of the past can affect how we view our future and its possibilities.

The Challenge of Automatic Choices

Think about your own experience. You continue to make choices until you find something that works for you. And as soon as you make a choice, by definition you have limited your options. You may continue to use that choice over and over because it has worked for you in the past. It becomes automatic, blocking some of the energy flow that would allow you to explore other and perhaps better options.

You begin to say, "This is the way to do it." If you do not remain thoughtful, it becomes the way you'll do it for the rest of your life. This blocks your energy and your creativity. It's the paradox of choice. It both moves you ahead and limits further choices with respect to that decision.

When a choice becomes automatic, it becomes limiting. You're no longer consciously making a choice.

> *(Julia)* It intrigues me that we create and embrace automatic choices, which are limits, yet most of us believe we don't want to be limited. The majority of the people I coach, consult for,

and teach immediately think of a "limit" as being negative. For example, when we're planning a strategy, they don't like the sound of "limiting the options."

Yet this does not have to be a bad thing. When we make a choice, we've taken a position. That position may be seen as the end of one choice and the beginning of another. Instead of seeing a limit as the end of the road, beyond which lies the dangerous unknown, we can see it as a border that we want to live within until it's time to explore new territory with new choices. This means that as soon as we've made a choice, we position ourselves to be open to new choices.

If we're thoughtful, when we come to one of our automatic limits, we will ask, "Are things the same as before, and therefore I will uphold the choice I've made, or has the context changed so that it's time to revisit the limit?"

Living at the Edge of Chaos

How can you, through activating your Thoughtful I, avoid operating from solely automatic choices? The answer to that question is: *By living at the edge of chaos, around the midpoint between equilibrium and chaos.*

In chaos theory, one extreme condition is equilibrium, and the other is total chaos. At the chaos extreme, there is no order, no memory, and nothing is precisely repeatable—everything appears random. Any patterns that form are invisible to the "naked eye." Conversely, at the equilibrium extreme, everything is organized and predictable and there is no movement.

Driven by the orientation of the mind, our tendency is to move toward—and try to remain within—equilibrium. Even the greatest lover of novelty among us still lives by patterns and habits set up by the choices we have made that have become automatic. Equilibrium seems safe to us. It is still, unchanging, knowable, and predictable. However, it stops us from growing. It stops us from being open to new possibilities.

Living at the edge of chaos does not mean living at the edge of an abyss. It means living in constant movement swinging either side of the midpoint between equilibrium and chaos. With our Thoughtful I operating in the border range of chaos, we allow ourselves to be open to new, creative ways and patterns of doing things (the chaos side), while still having memory and operating with the benefits of experience, of what worked in the past (the equilibrium side).

The creativity and excitement available at the edge of chaos encourages us to be aware, stay engaged, and be open to new understanding of our environment.

Thoughtful I = Thoughtful Eye

The Thoughtful I may also be considered the Thoughtful Eye, our window on the world. Researchers tell us that our minds operate in three-dimensional color pictures, and that we can create only a picture of "presence." We cannot imagine "lack."

To demonstrate this concept, we want you *not* to think of a pink elephant. What came into your mind just then? The *lack* of a pink elephant, or, much more likely, the pink pachyderm itself? Consider the implications of this the next time you tell your three-year-old daughter, "Take this glass of juice over to the table, and *don't spill it.*"

Making the
Thoughtful I
Work for You

The ongoing, primary goal of the Thoughtful I is to prevent you from living on automatic pilot through major chunks of your life.

It is interesting to observe some people living automatically in parts of their lives and not in others. For some, work becomes highly engaging, while family life is relegated to autopilot. For others, it's the other way around.

The critical point to remember is that **it's your choice.** If you are comfortable riding the wave of those "cherished beliefs," regardless of how limiting they may be, that's your choice. Hiding behind the statement, "Well, I can't do anything about it," is itself a choice.

We believe you really *can* do something about it—that it really is your choice.

A

AWARENESS

The
Thoughtful I
and Awareness
Your emotions do not simply present
themselves all on their own. They come from your thoughts, which have
been triggered by a stimulus.

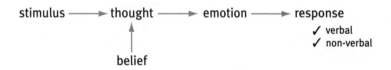

That stimulus may be something someone else has said or done, or it
could even come from one of your own thoughts about something.

The nature of the thought triggered by the stimulus is heavily influ-
enced by your beliefs—those shoulds and shouldn'ts and all the
structures you have built around yourself over time, whether they be reli-
gious, political, socio-economic, or family-related.

When there's a stimulus to the thought, an emotion follows. If it's a strong emotion, you are likely to respond quickly, and automatically: "Hey, that's a great idea!" or "How dare you say that!" The response may be positive or negative. Either way, it's automatic and emotion-based.

The Thoughtful I intervenes between emotion and response. The I becomes aware of the emotions we have and says, "Now, that's interesting. Why am I so positive about that? Negative about that? Neutral about that? Is there something I want to do about it? Do I want to continue to do it the same way or do I want to make a change?"

This section, on AWARENESS, explores these three practices:

- Stay Mindfully Aware
- Capture—and Cherish—Your Lightness
- Be Thoughtfully Authentic

2

Stay Mindfully Aware

This practice is all about focusing your awareness on the flow of personal energy. There are three horizons of this awareness:

- What's going on inside you.
- What's going on between you and another person.
- What's going on inside another person.

By understanding what's going on within you, you can manage your view of the situation and your interaction with others. By appreciating the way you and another are interacting—regardless of how you feel about the situation—you can take action to adjust your behavior and improve the energy flow between you. By observing that something is "going on" in another person that is interfering with their flow of energy, you can take steps either to understand their situation and facilitate the flow of energy, or bring the interaction to a close if it is unproductive.

Being Aware of Yourself

Mindful awareness begins with you. It begins with your becoming aware of how you react to your day-to-day experiences.

> *(Bob)* One morning I was driving my daughter to school. What is normally a 12-minute drive took 45 minutes. The trip from there to my first appointment of the day, which should have taken 20 minutes, took almost an hour.
>
> I could feel my frustration growing as I saw my back-to-back meetings fall like dominoes. I was then susceptible to being emotionally hijacked by the actions of drivers who tried to edge in front of me in a single lane of traffic.
>
> At one point, when I was behind a bus, a huge contractor's truck pulled up beside me and turned on his signal. The printable substance of what I was thinking was, "I'm not lettin' anybody in—I've let enough people in!"
>
> The standoff lasted about a minute and a half. When the driver finally figured out I wasn't going to move, he gunned his engine and swung into the line in front of the bus.
>
> It may have taken me awhile, but I did recognize that I was getting emotionally hijacked. Rather than adding everyone around me into the category of flaming idiots, I released that feeling. I laughed at myself, accessing the practice of Capture— and Cherish—Your Lightness (see chapter 3). So the meeting I was heading to was going to be a bit shorter because of my lateness. What did it matter, really? I called ahead, explained the situation, and then accepted the reality of the drive and enjoyed the ride.

> I realized the intensity of my emotion when I had to go back a track on the audio book I was listening to. I had missed most of it.

Staying mindfully aware means stepping outside the forces of the moment and checking in on yourself, assessing what's really happening to you.

Are circumstances affecting your normal, healthy way of being? Does your behavior match how you see yourself and how you'd want yourself to act in this situation? When you get hijacked, you get bogged down in negative feelings that prevent you from acting the way you'd like to. To find out what's really happening to you, pay attention to your breathing, posture, and muscle tension. Then ask yourself:

- *"What am I feeling right now?"*
- *"Am I still breathing, or am I holding my breath?"*
- *"Are my muscles tensing, or is my posture relaxed?"*

When you're not mindfully aware in this way, you don't know what's happening to you. You are propelled by your emotions. As mentioned earlier, the progression you go through in these situations starts with some *stimulus*—a statement by someone else, for example—that triggers an *automatic thought* in your mind that's based on some closely held *belief*, and the thought in turn triggers an *emotion* within you, and finally a verbal or non-verbal *response*.

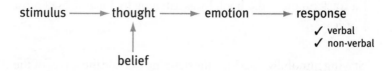

As soon as you become aware that you have a strong emotion rising—particularly a negative one—you have the choice to block the path between the automatic emotion and the automatic response, go back to thinking consciously about what's happening, and decide whether to change your thought about it, and thereby your emotion. Further, you may decide to explore the belief underlying that thought, choosing either to *change* that belief or *reinforce* it.

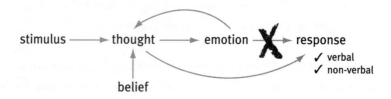

Learning to change your automatic thoughts is not necessarily straightforward. They can become so automatic that you're not even aware of them and only aware of the emotions they stir up. That strong emotion is your first clue.

(Bob) A close friend of ours has a teenager who often tests her resilience. She described a typical interchange to us.

As the story goes, while she was in the middle of preparing dinner, her daughter came into the kitchen with an agenda on her mind.

"I need to go to the sports store," she said. "Will you give me a ride over?"

The mother's immediate, though unspoken, reaction was, "Does it look like I'm not doing anything?"

Instead of responding automatically, she acknowledged the rather intense emotion to herself and quickly began to examine her thoughts and beliefs. She recognized that she had been thinking along the lines of, "You don't think what I have to do is as important as what you have to do. You're so insensitive"— an emotion of resentment.

So she changed her thought to, "You're focused on your own stuff and that's OK; we just need to understand that we both have needs and work to satisfy them both."

As a result, her thought generated a different emotion—one of acceptance—and she responded with, "Hey, girl, I hear you're anxious to get over to the store, and I'm in the middle of preparing dinner so we don't eat too late tonight. How can we work this out so it's good for both of us?"

The daughter now had the challenge of coming up with an answer and jumped in with, "OK, how about I help you prepare dinner for 15 minutes, then you take me over to the store while dinner's cooking?"

Confrontation avoided; mutually acceptable solution found; and a solid foundation created for future productive dialogue and relationships.

So, by changing your thought about something, you change the resulting emotion, your response to the situation, and the outcome.

Now if you choose *not* to change your thought about it and act through the original emotion, that's OK—it's your choice. At least now it's a conscious action rather than an automatic one.

The first part of being conscious in this way is to stay *mindfully* aware of all of your own states: physical, emotional, mental, and even spiritual. Put things into perspective. Ask yourself: "What does being half an hour late in traffic have to do with my life purpose? How important is it in the larger scheme of things?" This will allow you to settle down.

By staying mindfully aware, we can say, "This response is getting the better of me—I'm going to let it go."

> *(Julia)* I was on my way to lunch with a very close friend and a cousin of hers who was an acquaintance of mine. Having just wrapped up a meeting that had left me feeling angry, I arrived to find my two lunch companions already there and greeted them enthusiastically.
>
> When Heather, whom I had not seen in about 15 years, remarked that I looked the same as I had the last time she saw me, I launched into a description of an argument I had had with someone who had said I had a lot of gray hair.
>
> A couple of minutes into my story, Jacquie put her hand on my arm and said, "Whoa, slow down, girl! Why are you so hyper?"
>
> With her touch and her remark, Jacquie made me mindfully aware of how some stored emotions were affecting my energy. I thought I had been managing the anger, and yet my hyper energy was a clear indication that I was not. I acknowledged to my lunch partners the anger I had been feeling from my previ-

ous meeting and told them I was going to set it aside. I rolled my shoulders back, straightened my posture, took a deep breath, and, laughing, told them that my hairdresser called my gray hair "blonde highlights." The conversation proceeded at a leisurely and relaxed pace.

By not being mindfully aware of the state of my energy, I had jeopardized a lunch that had been months in the planning. I was thankful that Jacquie had been there to remind me of what I knew to do and had forgotten to do.

So when you feel yourself getting emotionally hijacked, you can either change your thought about it, along with the resulting emotion, or you can just let the emotion go for the moment. With the latter approach, it is important to come back later and explore the emotion, the thoughts, and the underlying beliefs to help avoid getting hijacked the next time.

Being Aware of Blocks to Interpersonal Energy

The second part of staying mindfully aware is being attentive to what may be blocking the flow of energy in interactions with others. The objective here is to sense when someone has something going on that's dampening the energy between you. That "something" could be what's going on within you or the other person, or it could be something in your immediate environment.

Even, or maybe especially, when you are in a dialogue with somebody—whether with a spouse, child, business colleague, or client—the first step is still to stay aware of yourself. If you are trying to be empathetic, trying to persuade, or trying to accomplish something in that dialogue, you need the energy to flow. That means you need to be aware of things that are going to block your interpersonal energy. The source of these blocks may be physical, like a cold or a headache. They may be mental or emotional, like a disturbing conversation you've just had with a spouse. Or they may be environmental, like excessive noise or heat.

Whatever the case, ask yourself how the potential block may affect your interaction with others. If it is affecting your health, your state of mind, or your state of physical well-being, expend some extra effort to get yourself engaged to improve the energy flow, or work to mitigate the blocks.

> *(Bob)* I am president of an association in Toronto and was chairing our winter meeting in the midst of a terrible headache. I had to continually catch my mind drifting off either to thoughts unrelated to the meeting or to the pain itself. I needed to give myself some relief and still keep the energy of the meeting going. At one point I said to a fellow board member, "OK, Clark, this is your area. For the next 10 minutes, the meeting's yours."
>
> By delegating part of the meeting to him, I was able to take advantage of another member's strengths and to inject new energy into the meeting. I was also able to conserve what was left of my energy in order to concentrate on the overall flow of the meeting. My Thoughtful I had reminded me that complaining about my headache would be "all about me" and would block my own and everyone else's energy. Mindful awareness brought about a much better result.

There's no denying that it requires work to adopt and follow the practices that we're describing in this book. It would be easier for you to continue to do what you have always done. It would be easier for you, having tried something new and finding it a challenge, to flip back into the old behaviors.

Our experience has convinced us that if more of us practiced being mindfully aware of just our own feelings, it would make an enormous difference in the world. And looking one step beyond that, if more of us were able to function at the level of understanding the interplay between people, we would then have the tools to begin to truly expand the energy that flows between people.

Working with Blockages in Others

The third level of awareness is seeing another person's energy being blocked and thus having an impact on the interchange between you and them.

When you become aware of a blockage in another, you have two choices:

- You can suspend the conversation and explore what's going on in the other person and the impact it's having on the dialogue.
- Or you can wind up the conversation and defer it to a later time.

At this point in our analysis, behavior, not cause, is the concern. You don't need to be a psychologist or a social worker to resolve the situation. The beauty of the Energy Exchange method is that it's both behavior-based and thought-based.

> *(Bob)* Like many other couples, my wife and I can sense quickly when something's not quite right between us, and it's usually because each of us is in a different space or mood. I'm quiet and she's exuberant, or vice versa, or I'm feeling a little down and she's "over the moon," or vice versa. It's at those times that the energy does not flow smoothly between us and we each recognize it and work to adjust the energy flow, or move out of the situation.
>
> It takes the Thoughtful I in both of our minds to make the required adjustments, to keep us from reacting automatically and contributing to a mound of sludge that could build up between us.

Many people think the key to such situations is to explore with the other person what is causing them to react in a dysfunctional manner. From the perspective of energy flow, however, the origins and content of the feelings don't matter to you. The goal for you and others is simply to stop any behavior blocking the flow of personal energy and the energy of the discussion.

It's important for you to understand the strength of the mind-body connection and the ways in which the body does things we're not aware of. Our fight-or-flight responses are direct and physical, one of the automatic responses controlled by the amygdala in the brain.

Daniel Goleman, who pioneered the theory of emotional intelligence, writes that if we are more aware of our thoughts and their impact, we'll have more opportunity to control our responses. In other words, we take charge of our responses, and not the other way around.

In some situations, all you can do is focus on the behavior. Maybe what's inside blocking the person is something only a psychologist or psychiatrist can work with. However, knowing the source of the problem would be able to make the exchange all the better. If you care about the person and the relationship, it may be worth taking the time to reach a shared understanding of the source of the blockage.

You can help others be mindfully aware of themselves if there is trust and permission for you to do so. The prerequisite is the creation of a safe environment in which the individual can say things openly without fear of invalidation. The absence of fear enables the flow of creative energy.

The goal is to become mindfully aware of what may be operating within the person that's causing their energy to get blocked. Sometimes you can get to this point through dialogue. This kind of exchange can take place with a spouse, a child, a friend.

With the help of your Thoughtful I, you can learn to become more and more mindfully aware of what's happening inside and around you. As your awareness deepens, you can use it to improve your communications and your relationships.

3

Capture—and Cherish—Your Lightness

We have been discussing how important it is for you to be aware of when you're being emotionally hijacked. We've also been exploring the *stimulus* → *automatic thought/belief* → *emotion* → *response* sequence that so often gets us into trouble. Now, in this chapter, we'll consolidate this understanding in order to help you learn to capture and cherish your lightness. By "lightness" we mean your ability to keep from getting hijacked in the first place and your ability to keep the energy flowing both within yourself and between you and others.

Capturing and cherishing your lightness requires you to check your ego at the door. When your ego gets in the way, your intensity escalates. When you get intense, it's as if your density increases. This density blocks the flow of your own energy and certainly can get in the way of an energy exchange.

There are five major emotions that trigger emotional hijacking. We call them the ARGUE emotions:

- *Anger*
- *Resentment*
- *Guilt*
- *Unworthiness*
- *Embarrassment*

The normal physical response associated with the ARGUE emotions is shallow breathing, leading to a feeling of suffocation. It's also a heaviness, a feeling of being swamped by an emotional response to a situation, which may cause a feeling of tightness in your chest. Your breathing becomes shallow, and you feel as if you are "sinking below the water" of your experience. If you're able to prevent the ARGUE emotions from taking over, you can stay

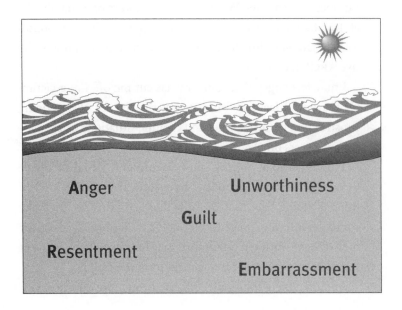

above the water, where you feel lighter and more buoyant. Above the waterline, it's so much easier for energy and positive feelings to flow.

ARGUE happens differently for different people, based on their personal histories and the resulting unique patterns of stimulus triggers and responses. A given situation or stimulus will obviously generate a different thought and emotional response in different people. That's why it's so important for you to be mindfully aware of your thoughts and emotions as you respond to situations and the stimuli inherent in them.

> *(Bob)* I've been doing a lot of the city driving in our family lately, dropping off and picking up. I've noticed that when I'm driving along and someone cuts in front of me, I have one of a number of responses. What I've become aware of is that they're all fear-based, related to the primitive fight-or-flight responses to a threatening situation. I end up having one or more of the five ARGUE emotions.
>
> I may feel **angry** that someone has cut me off. I'm a victim. Or maybe I'll feel **anger** directed at the city for always doing construction in the summer and creating situations where people cut others off. Another victim response.
>
> This anger may "morph" into **resentment**. "If I didn't have to do this driving, I wouldn't have to deal with this kind of thing. I should have told Dorothy that I couldn't do this. Why couldn't we have arranged a car pool? This is not a good day for me." If the resentment builds up, I may find myself trying to cut someone else off in order to get ahead in the traffic.
>
> And then there's the **guilt**. "If I had been more directive with

our daughter and got her out of bed, we would have left earlier, and I wouldn't be so concerned about someone getting in front of me." Or "What's the matter with me—if I had been concentrating on my driving, there wouldn't have been enough space in front of me for that guy to cut in." Or "Oh no, now we're going to be really late."

If I go far enough underwater, I may find myself having feelings of **unworthiness**. I may say, "I can't believe how stupid I am—I should have seen that coming. I should be concentrating more on my driving. I can't do anything right"—letting that voice take over until I feel overwhelmed. Now, not only has someone cut in front of me, but I'm feeling emotionally hijacked by a driver I don't even know!

Embarrassment could arise as well. I may reflect that I have not been concentrating on my driving and have caused someone else to take an action they normally would not take. Or, being proud of my driving skills, I may feel mortified that I made a learner's mistake.

This rather banal example is set up just to make distinctions between the five emotions. Faced with such a situation, you may well have one particular emotion that you habitually call up.

These ARGUE responses, in addition to dampening your energy, can have a profound effect on your emotions and physical well-being. And they can build up, causing ulcers, chronic headaches, and all manner of serious illnesses.

As soon as you become mindfully aware of that emotional hijacking, you have a choice. You can wallow in it, be a victim, and continue to feel angry, resentful, guilty, unworthy, or embarrassed.

Even more powerfully, as highlighted in chapter 2, you can revisit your thought—and perhaps the underlying belief—and change your thought. That generates a different emotion, one that is lighter and encourages the flow of energy.

The emotions that reflect this lightness are the TOGA emotions:

Trust
Optimism
Gratitude
Acceptance

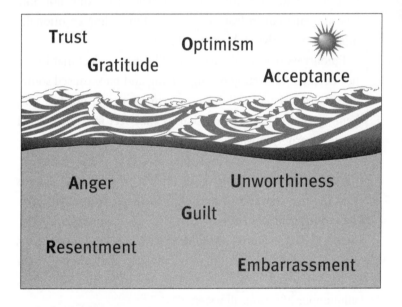

How to Lighten Up

You will find it fairly easy to recognize when the ARGUE response is happening. You will feel it somewhere in your body. In addition to the shallow breathing we mentioned earlier, it may be a knot in your stomach or a sense that your shoulders are about to touch your ears. It may be a feeling that a steel band is tightening around your head. Whatever the signal your body gives you, you have a choice about the response you make. You can continue to ARGUE, or you can capture and cherish your lightness—or "lighten up," for short.

Becoming en*light*ened by choosing to practice capturing and cherishing your lightness requires three steps.

First, return to the practice of staying mindfully aware. Staying mindfully aware of your body will allow you to recognize what's happening in your mind.

Second, shift from me to I. Once you have identified that the ARGUE emotions are at work, you will realize that you are focusing on yourself and that somehow you have become the only actor in the situation. It's all about "me."

Reflect on the words, "It's not all about me." Using the vowels of personal power means understanding that in a powerful sense we're all one, all part of the same system. You matter—and so does everyone else. Remember the story above about being cut off in traffic? Perhaps the other driver was in a hurry, too, rushing to the hospital to see a family member, for example. Perhaps the other driver had not been concentrating on driving and made a mistake that they immediately regretted. We may never know what was going on for the other person. What we do know is that in the larger scheme of things, this particular situation is not likely to be the "make it or break it" experience of our lives.

Third, look for the ways you have attempted to "lighten up" a difficult situation in the past—a situation where your energy was blocked or the energy flow between you and others was blocked. Most of us have developed these coping mechanisms and we need to become more mindfully aware of them and the impact they have on the situations we are attempting to remedy.

Some people use humor to find their own lightness and allow the energy to flow. Some people use deep breathing to recapture their lightness. In all cases, as far as we can tell, it involves what Rosamund and Benjamin Zander, in their book *The Art of Possibility*, call Rule #6.

> *(Bob)* The Zanders tell the story of a meeting between two prime ministers. They're about five minutes into their in-camera dialogue when an aide comes in fuming about something that's gone awry. The host prime minister says, "Remember, Peter, Rule #6." Peter immediately calms down, apologizes, and leaves. This happens three more times. Finally the visiting prime minister says, "Excuse me, Prime Minister, I must find out about this Rule #6. It sounds very powerful."
>
> "Oh, it's quite simple," the PM says. "Rule #6 is, 'Don't take yourself so @#$% seriously.'"
>
> "Oh, that's a wonderful rule," he responds. "I think that would be useful in my country as well. What are the other rules?"
>
> "There aren't any!" the PM answers.

Take the Issue—and Not Yourself—Seriously

There's an important distinction to be made between taking an issue or a situation seriously and taking yourself too seriously. The goal here is for you to learn to let go of emotional responses and behaviors that distract you from the really important concerns of the moment. To do that, you have to learn to take yourself less seriously in the larger context of the universe.

(Bob) A few summers back, we were at our family cottage for a couple of weeks, and were informed that a water line had broken and flooded our house back in the city. Not good.

I called the insurance company and arranged for an adjuster to enter the building to assess the damage so I could begin making arrangements for repair. I didn't want to interrupt my holiday, so we stayed at the cottage through the end of another week. That was particularly important to my wife and daughter.

I telephoned my older brother and told him about the situation and what I had done, and he said to me, "Bob, are you taking this seriously?" He had been ready to fly up to the house to see what he could do to help.

I responded with, "Well, what would I do differently if I were on-site?" I had already released my thoughts concerning, "I should have turned off the water at the main tap," and "I should have replaced all those faulty connections when I had the opportunity."

In this case, I was able to take the issue seriously, while accepting "what's done is done," and stay relatively light within myself, accepting that I was doing what needed to be done.

This doesn't mean, of course, that you're not going to take your relationships and work seriously. Rather, it means that you're going to be more flexible and open to the ideas of others because you know you don't have all the answers. As we'll explore later in the book, you'll become better able to stay resolved in situations without being attached to ego concerns.

(Julia) It's this kind of approach that now makes it easy for me to accept feedback from people on the various committees I sit on in my community. While this feedback *is* personal in that it's feedback that I triggered, it's not about my essence. Again, it's not about me—it's about I and them. It's feedback about what we did or said, not feedback about who we are.

If I take the feedback seriously without taking myself too seriously, then I can make changes to what I do in order to become more effective. That's going to make me feel good about myself. And my energy will be much more positive and contagious than if I take it personally and start thinking negative thoughts about my capability.

At the same time, I take my volunteer work seriously and do my best to make my contributions useful. I attempt to do it with a light step—after all, the world can be fixed only one small step at a time (an old saying that helps me put things in perspective).

Now, it's inevitable that the person giving me the feedback will sometimes be "on a mission." They will have too much ego involved in expressing that opinion and may be somewhat aggressive or unkind in getting their point across. In that case, it's even more important that I stay mindfully aware in order not to be emotionally hijacked by the feedback.

When your ego is strongly identified with the issue in question, the situation is more complex. Your density increases and your energy becomes blocked. It's harder to be creative about solutions when you feel the problem has its root in your values and cherished beliefs.

(Bob) As a parent, I find I'm often put into situations where my ego gets too involved and I want to control the situation.

When my daughter does something I don't want her to do, such as start to play on my laptop computer beside the desktop computer I'm diligently working on, I can feel myself getting more intense. I want to say. "Can't you see how hard I am working? Can't you find somewhere else to play?"

The important goal in this kind of situation is to be mindfully aware and identify the source of that response. If I can do that, I can lighten up and find a more appropriate response.

So I pause and acknowledge that I feel this strong reaction coming on. I take a deep breath and send the ARGUE emotions away. I now feel lighter and it's easier for me to assess what's happening. She was taking me away from something I wanted to do—and what I wanted to do was no more important than what she wanted to do—to be with Daddy. So, I change my thought about it, set the work aside, and get more personally engaged with her. I'll come back to what I was doing later, with renewed energy.

When you get locked into a condition where it's all about *me*, your focus goes inward. Again, picture an object caught in a black hole, getting denser and denser and denser—before long, the energy just can't flow. If you blow apart that condition of heavy gravity, the energy can flow again and be more creative in its flow.

When you're en*light*ened—when you're mindfully aware of how you are coming across to others and how people are receiving you; when you're being authentic, and being thoughtful about that authenticity—your own energy can flow again. This means that the energy is flowing between you and others around you. You can see that you're having a really positive impact on the energy flow and the success of yourself and others.

In the next chapter, we'll look at how awareness can help you know how and when to express your true feelings to others.

4

Be Thoughtfully Authentic

Chapters 2 and 3 dealt with being mindfully aware, both of yourself and how your energy is flowing and of others and how their energy and yours are working together. We also saw what enables and fuels this process—the practice of taking a more cheerful approach to life.

Now, in this chapter, let's look at how you can be thoughtfully authentic—truthful with yourself and others about the feelings you are having. In being thoughtfully authentic, you determine when and how to share what you feel.

When and How to Share Your Feelings

We've all known people who are blunt yet who don't express their feelings thoughtfully—there's no filter between mind and mouth. Recalling these people is a useful reminder that in our attempts to be authentic, we have to be careful not to be *thoughtlessly* authentic.

You can get into trouble when you don't consciously mediate between stimulus and response. Something upsets you, and *boom!* You snap at those close to you: "Who do you think you are to say that? What you just said is rude and inappropriate!" All this originates from your own history of what worked and didn't work for you, your shoulds and shouldn'ts, and some fears you picked up along the way. If you can get past these automatic responses, everything will work more smoothly for you.

Being authentic is not a matter of "letting it all hang out" and telling people everything about how you're feeling. It has much more to do with dealing with the energy in the moment. So instead of just telling people what you think and feel, you work with other people, with real, genuine interest in your mutual success. You work with them to make sure you are telling each other the truths you need to know in order to move forward.

Staying mindfully aware is the starting point (if you do only that, it will get you a long way), along with capturing and cherishing your lightness. Now, to be thoughtfully authentic, you must move on in the relationship on the basis of observation. You can say, "Now let me make a choice about how I'm going to communicate what I feel."

> *(Bob)* In the past I tended to share very quickly what I was feeling, because I hadn't yet started thinking about the feelings. I remember a conversation I had with my wife.
>
> We were just sitting around one evening after dinner. We had been discussing a family friend and some concerns my wife had about her.
>
> "I think that she is really playing the victim," Dorothy said.
>
> "That's a rather judgmental statement," I said, really without

thinking too much about what I was saying.

"So is that!" she replied, with some force behind her words.

I could feel the energy flow getting interrupted between us. Becoming mindfully aware, I realized that I had caused that quick energy blockage. With a flippant comment, I had criticized Dorothy and shut her down, instead of letting her express herself. I needed to take immediate action to defuse the situation.

"Yeah, you're right," I said. "Sorry. Please go on with what you were saying."

By staying mindfully aware and being thoughtfully authentic, I was able to rephrase my response. So in such situations, I can say, "Hey, that's an interesting thought. Tell me more. Tell me what that opinion is based on." This is much better than saying something like, "That's judgmental." Dorothy was right. That was itself a judgmental statement.

My next task switches to using another practice, which is *confirming my understanding* of why my wife may have reached this conclusion. (This practice is the subject of chapter 13.)

The Buddhists have a great piece of advice that applies to these situations—to simply ask yourself three questions in any situation before responding: "Is it true? Is it useful? It is kind?"

(Bob) As a constantly giving person, my wife gets caught up in starting new projects—sculpting statues as gifts for friends, writing poems for special occasions, or getting involved in programs at our daughter's school. She has much more on the go than time to do them. Then she gets frustrated, becoming overwhelmed by the backlog. As both a witness to this, and

someone who feels the impact, I struggle with the best way to address the situation.

Using the questions of the Buddhists, I ask myself what part of the situation is true. Well, I can see there's more stuff to do than time to do them, and I see the frustration in her demeanor and hear it in her voice. I also recognize my feeling of concern as I see its impact on her health—being tired, experiencing more severe headaches—and on our daughter and me in terms of being around that kind of energy.

Is what I have to say useful? I know it will be useful only when she's ready to hear it. That will require a judgment on my part and must be considered in terms of her needs rather than mine.

And can I express it in a kind way? We're all different in how we go about this, and for me, my observations need to be put into a context of what she's trying to accomplish with her life, without any judgment about what she needs to do about it, and with a lot of love and caring in my voice and eyes.

I find this takes a lot of conscious effort. I understand that it's better to engage my energy in this way than to let things fester inside, and it's certainly a lot better than reacting automatically.

It's About I

An ongoing theme of this book is that one of the keys to being thoughtfully authentic is to use "I language." For example, instead of, "You have made me feel unloved," it's, "When you say that, I feel unloved."

Using "I language" keeps the conversation going. You avoid blaming the other person, because that works against the flow of energy and tends to turn a dialogue into a confrontation. Using I language gives the other person a way out, rather than waving a red flag and forcing them to charge back.

(Julia) My friend Colleen told me about some interactions she had with her daughter Erica when Erica was 15 or 16.

Erica would sometimes come home from school and make disrespectful comments to Colleen—"You're a loser," "I hate this ugly house," "We never have anything good to eat."

Now, how does a parent respond to that? I think a lot of parents would have said, "You do not speak to me in that tone of voice!" This, of course, would have the effect of silencing Erica or of increasing her abusiveness. In either case, the dialogue will not move forward.

A statement such as, "You make me feel unloved" is no better. It lays blame, and the most obvious response is, "You shouldn't feel unloved." What use is that?

Colleen's approach when Erica made one of these disrespectful comments was to say, "Hearing you say that makes me feel sad. It makes me think that you're upset about something. Why not tell me what's happened?"

Being thoughtfully authentic means saying, "Let me tell you what I felt when you said that." This approach keeps the energy flowing and invites the other person to consider what's happening inside them and respond in a thoughtful way.

(Bob) What's also interesting is that many people use "you language" that distances themselves *from* their own selves. When talking about a problem they have, many will say something

like, "Well, when you're faced with having to make that choice, you'll always take the one that preserves the family."

Of course, what the person is actually describing is their *own* behavior, not *your* behavior. They are really saying, "Well, when I'm faced with having to make that choice, I always take the one that preserves the family."

Our advice is to use I language to help you stay mindfully aware of what you are thinking and feeling. Speaking this language gives you a greater opportunity to be authentic.

Notice what happens inside when you use I language. The Thoughtful I tells you that you are choosing to think what you are thinking and to feel what you are feeling. Remembering that it's about I and not about me allows you to take responsibility for your own responses.

Choosing Kinder Language

In any interaction, the energy flows best when you are careful to avoid language that hijacks others emotionally. Some of your ways of casually relating to others may be unintentionally confrontational or guilt-inducing.

It's important to stay mindfully aware of the language you use and how it affects other people. The words you choose can hijack others and block energy. How? By generating anger back at you, resentment that you're doing something harmful to them, or feelings of guilt, unworthiness, or embarrassment that you or they haven't acted in a certain way.

You can consciously change the words you use, getting rid of:

- *Shoulds* and *shouldn'ts.*
- *But* (try "and" instead!).
- *Guilt-imposing questions* such as, "Why didn't you…?", "Why wouldn't you?", and "Why don't you?"

Let's look at each one of these.

Stop Shoulding on People

The words "should" and "shouldn't" are two of the strongest stimuli for explosive emotions.

> *(Bob)* We have a close friend whom we love dearly and who is strongly opinionated. In our early days of being parents, he was constantly observing our parenting style and the opportunities we were giving our daughter, and continued to make comments when we got together for dinner. Such as, "You know, you really should send your daughter to *x* independent school."
>
> When these comments came out, I'd catch myself getting emotionally hijacked, thinking, "On what basis does *he* know what school would be good for our daughter?" I'd have to work very hard to come back to my Thoughtful I and release that emotion.
>
> So, knowing the impact of this on me, I try to be very careful in the wording I use when I pass advice on to others. I know I would have responded much more easily to, "You know, you might find *x* independent school a good match for your daughter."
>
> Oh, the power of words.

When you say to someone, "Well, what you should do is this..." it's difficult for them not to get hijacked. They are immediately forced to jump to their own defense: "You have no understanding of what I'm going through. What gives you the right...?" Getting rid of the shoulds and shouldn'ts from your vocabulary will be a powerful contributor to energy flow.

The Importance of But-ing Out

The little word "but" is insidious in our language. In the Oxford dictionary, its definitions consume 28 lines. Most of the meanings have to do with contrasting two things that cannot, or do not, exist in the same place, like "everything but the kitchen sink."

When you use the word "but" in conversation—and most often, automatically—you are likely believing that you're stating a contrary view. For example: "I hear what you're saying we should do about this situation, but we've never been able to make that approach work here."

In this case, "but" is an inaccurate conjunction, since the suggested course of action and the fact that "we've never been able to make it work here" are both valid and in the same space.

The insidious part is what it does to the flow of energy. By and large, the effect of the "but" is to negate and replace the stated idea with one's own view of the world.

Listen to the subtle difference of replacing the "but" with "and" in this sentence: "I hear what you're saying we should do about this situation, *and* we've never been able to make that approach work here."

Through this kind of statement, you can acknowledge that both statements are valid and in the same space. And the energy now has a better chance of being applied. The response now can be, "Well, then, what might we do to make the approach work in this environment?"

So here's our advice. Every time you feel the little but-word coming up your throat, change it to an "and" before letting it come out of your mouth, and see what impact that has on the energy in the dialogues you're having.

By the way, this rule applies even when you're doing your own thinking about something. When that "but" rears, replace it with an "and" and see if the meaning of what you're thinking about changes, and see what happens to your own energy flow.

> *(Julia)* I remember one night last summer my son asked us if he could go out with his friends. Knowing that he had to go to work the next morning, I said, "You can go out, but remember that you have an early day tomorrow."
>
> What was the point of my using "but"? It set up an implied conflict between his activities that night and his work obligations the next day; it also implied, perhaps, that I thought he was being irresponsible by going out.
>
> Looking back, I wish I'd but-ed out. I should have said yes, and left it at that. If I really felt I needed to remind him about work (not that he would ever have forgotten), I could have brought it up as a separate point.

Avoid Guilt-inducing Questions

In somewhat the same way that "but" has grown to have an impact so much larger than its size, the word "why" can also have a negative impact on energy flow. Asking "why" often has the effect of stimulating an ARGUE response.

(Julia) The other day a colleague asked me, "Why didn't you put the new information up on the website?" My immediate response was to feel angry. "Because I had to do so much editing" was what I wanted to say.

I quickly realized, however, that he probably wasn't trying to make me feel guilty. In fact, he was feeling insecure about some text he'd written for the site. He was afraid his poor work had been the cause of a delay.

Very often, when someone asks a question that causes an ARGUE response, there's something else going on that you need to find out about. By being thoughtfully authentic, you'll encourage energy flow instead of blocking it.

The "why didn't you" and "why wouldn't you" phrases set up two dynamics that work against the free flow of energy:

- The first dynamic is that these questions imply, "You haven't considered all the alternatives, whereas *I* can easily see other options." This can come across as condescending to the person dealing with the matter at hand.
- The second is that these questions ask you to identify the negatives—why it *wouldn't* work—hijacking the discussion into a defense of why that option has not been surfaced before, laced with the guilt of not having been smart enough to think it through.

You can try more positive and powerful, and less inflammatory phrases, such as, "Have you considered doing …?" and "How about doing …?"

Encouraging Dialogue

Let's think about authenticity in dialogues.

If you have any sense that someone is not being authentic with you, your willingness to trust them is reduced. You become more guarded. You don't share yourself completely. This limits the energy between you.

The first step, in such a situation, is not for you to try to get the other person to be authentic. The first step is to be authentic yourself. As Gandhi said, "Be the change you want in the world."

Instead of blaming the other person for the blockage, remember that it's not all about me, it's about I. So you may say, "I am feeling right now that you're holding something back," or, "I have the feeling that you're not giving me the whole story. I'm not sure if that's true or not; it's just the feeling I have. Is there something else I need to know?"

> *(Bob)* I had an experience with my wife that rocked me back on my heels.
>
> I had been traveling on client assignments a great deal, was away from home a lot, and when I was at home was tied up both with client work and the writing of this book. At one point in one of my assignments, I had to fly to Barbados to interview a client executive. When I mentioned it, Dorothy said, "Well, I'm coming on *that* trip!"
>
> I grabbed onto this idea because I realized it would allow us to reconnect and get some private time together in a delightful environment. So I worked to set up flights and accommodations. However, because of the short lead time, I was unable to get reasonable flights there and back without a huge hassle and great expense.

When I announced that I hadn't been able to "make it happen," something changed in Dorothy's demeanor. For a couple of days, I felt an intense and terrifying energy field around her, and also sensed that it was directed at me.

When I get into these situations, I get very uncomfortable speaking up—I'm afraid of the reaction I'll get if I do. So I decided to write her a note.

I worked on the note for a long time—perhaps a couple of hours—editing it on my computer to get it "just right" before handwriting it on notepaper. In the message I described the energy field I was experiencing, confirmed my deep love for her, and asked for some time when we could talk so I could better understand what was going on. When I finished the note, I placed it on the dining room table and raced out of the house for fear of any confrontation.

The result was magical. Not easy, mind you, and still magical. When we sat down, unencumbered by other bodies, Dorothy was able to get out into the open all the feelings she was having around her role as wife, mother, and dog walker (we have two demanding Golden Retrievers). She was feeling both spent and unvalued.

As we both concentrated on being thoughtfully authentic, we were able to clean out the silt that had been building up for months and reestablish a sound loving connection. As for the Barbados trip, it's still in the planning.

When you're in a situation like this you can say, "I'm being authentic with you in this exchange and it would be great if you were authentic with me, too."

There will always be times when other people refuse to be

authentic. Many people—for of a wide range of cultural, genetic, or environmental reasons—will choose to hide behind their veils. You cannot control another person's authenticity; you can only encourage them to be as authentic as they are willing to be.

And in the end, the greatest importance is for you to be authentic, regardless of what others do. Being Thoughtfully Authentic allows your own energy to flow more easily, keeping your energy channels free of the sludge that can work to make you physically, if not mentally and emotionally, ill.

In closing, remember that you do not need to be brutal to be authentic. Preset your mind with an emotion of caring and acceptance, and share how you feel.

Making Awareness Work for You

The foregoing practices, which enhance your ability to maintain your level of awareness, may be used in different ways, depending on what works for you as an individual. We certainly apply them differently.

> *(Bob)* The main idea for me in the awareness dimension is the observation of and management of emotional hijacking. By staying mindfully aware of my emotional level, I continually check whether I'm above or below the waterline. Am I feeling the ARGUE emotions of anger against someone or something? Resentment of someone? Guilt about something I've done? Unworthiness concerning my condition? Or embarrassment about something I've said?
>
> And if so, I move into changing my thoughts to reflect the TOGA emotions: trusting the other person or the situation, and then feeling optimism regarding the outcome, gratitude to myself or others or the situation, and acceptance.

I can then be thoughtfully authentic with myself and others and work to build a better understanding of my own beliefs—both the ones that are working for me and those that are limiting me.

Finally, I can change my thoughts—if I want to—and lighten up.

This self-awareness and other-awareness embrace the first steps to regaining dominion over my own mental, emotional, physical, and spiritual health.

(Julia) For me, awareness means staying in touch with my automatic thoughts. I have physical feelings associated with the automatic thoughts that generate ARGUE emotions. Now, whenever I have one of those feelings, I look for the automatic thought. More often than not, I find myself thinking "it's all about me."

So I take a few deep breaths and remind myself that I need to lighten up. The breathing gives my Thoughtful I the opportunity to create or access other thoughts that I could have about what's happening. Having engaged my Thoughtful I puts me in a position where I can honestly and authentically express myself in a way that encourages rather than blocks the energy flow.

What's been wonderful about my increasing awareness is that I have been able to develop a new set of automatic thoughts. These new thoughts generate good feelings for me and enable me to maintain my sense of perspective. I'm able to walk with a lighter step in the world, and I get much better results.

So how do you begin adopting these three practices to enhance your awareness? We understand that there's a lot to think about.

Start by just checking in with yourself every so often and asking the questions:

• Am I aware
... of what's going on inside me?
... between me and others?
... inside others?
• How do I know?

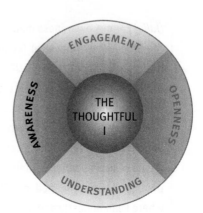

Then, if you're not satisfied with the answers, think about which of the three practices would be most useful to you in enhancing your awareness.

ENGAGEMENT

The Thoughtful I and Engagement

The Thoughtful I is engaged, and the very first sense of that is being *personally* engaged. Most people think that's wrong—that engagement means something like, "Hey, I'm a really good listener." Rather, personal engagement is, fundamentally:

> *Hey, I'm here. All of me is here for you and I am here physically, mentally, emotionally, and spiritually in favor of this engagement.*
>
> *I'm engaged in an outcome, personal or professional, understanding that the outcome could be realized in many different ways. I'm open to your thoughts on the matter. I know that by being fully engaged in the result that I'm trying to create, you will get excited, too, and help me along the way.*
>
> *We are all interdependent. My success, whether personal or professional, is intertwined with your success. So*

I know it's in my best interest to know what success is for you and to do what I can to help you succeed.

This section of the book, on the vowel of engagement, deals with these three practices:

- Get—and Stay—Engaged
- Stay Resolved Without Attachment
- Accept and Support Your Mutuality

5

Get — and Stay — Engaged

What happens to you, what you achieve in your life, is dictated less by your *abilities* than by the *choices* you make, including choices to do nothing.

One choice you make over and over again, day in and day out, whether you know it or not, is whether to be engaged with yourself and those around you.

Have you ever found yourself coming back from a "mind vacation" you hardly knew you were on? You may have wondered why you found yourself not listening to your child or spouse, mother or father, colleague or boss, even though you thought you were really focused on the conversation.

The answer is simple. You have more processing power in your mind than is required for listening to others. So you have lots of "cycles" left over to process other information, and that information can come from anywhere. In fact, it's pretty easy to be only half there in many situations when you have all this processing power sitting unused. That's why getting and staying engaged takes so much energy.

In the first section of this book, you saw how important it is to have your Thoughtful I at work to help you develop your awareness. Now you're ready to take the next step and look at how you engage with your world. In these next three chapters, you'll learn to concentrate on staying *engaged* with yourself and with others every day. Doing this improves your relationships, helps you get more out of every situation, and ensures an effective exchange of energy.

It Starts with You, Yourself, and Your Thoughtful I

To understand the practice of getting and staying engaged, consider what happens when you are by yourself.

Whether you're working or meditating or riding a bike, you know when you are engaged. You feel completely there and you can feel your own energy flow. In the same way, you know when you aren't completely there—usually after the fact. If you are going to get and stay engaged, and as a result maximize your own energy, then you have to check in on your engagement regularly.

Everyone has experienced difficulty starting a project. You've no doubt found yourself becoming distracted while working on something on your own. When that happens, your energy is blocked and it's hard for you to be creative, to create *anything*—in other words, it's hard to get anything done.

> *(Bob)* I find at times that it takes me a long time to get into whatever it is that I'm supposed to be working on. It can be any number of things getting in the way of engagement. I may be

preoccupied with something else that needs to be dealt with. It could simply be that I'm not set up physically to do what I want to do—I need to turn the heat up, or get a fresh cup of coffee.

What's important is for me to be mindfully aware of what's happening, and to be thoughtfully authentic about how I'm dealing with the situation. I've learned to accept the fact that sometimes it just takes a little longer to get engaged, and I cut myself some slack. I have also recognized that if it's taking too long, there's probably a better way for me to spend my time, and I find something else to do where I can be fully engaged. And I go back to the other task later.

(Julia) It's one thing to *get* engaged when you're on your own. And then there's the challenge of *staying* engaged.

When I started to work out of a home office, I found it was very easy to become disengaged from what I was doing. The phone rings, the mail arrives, the plant on my desk starts to look really thirsty—the list of potential distractions seems endless. Not to mention email!

So I set up some rules of engagement for myself to ensure that I could be productive. I set the phone to "no ring" and decided I would do email twice in the morning and twice in the afternoon. I scheduled regular breaks for myself to do things like water the plants, check voicemail, or get involved in some physical activity like stretching.

By staying mindfully aware of my need for structure, and by accepting that need without any ARGUEing, I was much better able to get and stay *personally* engaged.

Engaging with Others

We've talked about how you can stay *self*-engaged. It gets somewhat more complex when you engage with others. That's because the degree to which you get and stay engaged with those others is going to affect the energy exchange between you and the others—and therefore the result that you're working toward.

The degree to which you get and stay engaged with others also affects the relationship you have and are going to continue to have (or not) with those others. Here's where the ability to monitor and manage your engagement becomes critical. Not surprisingly, it takes energy to do this. When you use your energy to engage, you enable the flow of positive energy between yourself and others.

> *(Julia)* When our son was about 18 months old and I was work-ing part-time, I often found myself thinking about other things when I was playing with him. He would notice it before I did, and tell me—in one way or another—that he was not happy with me. He could tell, even if I *said* I was watching him do somersaults, that I wasn't really focused on him and his somer-saults.
>
> I realized that I would have to work on staying fully engaged with him, to keep from jeopardizing my integrity as a parent. So I started consciously checking in with myself to see how engaged I was. It was ironic, of course, that the very check-in I was doing meant that I was disengaging for a moment. I began to notice that I actually felt physically different when I was fully engaged with him, and it therefore became much easier for me to tell when I was beginning to disengage.
>
> This prompted me to start checking in with myself in other

situations. I found that getting and staying engaged required a high degree of mindful awareness. I had to *mean* it when I said I was paying attention—and if I wasn't able to be authentic about that, it meant I needed to do something differently. I could feel the change in my energy as I began to truly engage.

Whether you are engaging or you're disengaging, what's important is that you are making a choice, conscious or not. Thinking back to the basic premise of The Energy Exchange, you see how the degree of your engagement either accelerates or dissipates the flow of energy.

Increasing Your Engagement

What, then, can you do to make the right choice—to get and stay engaged and make that as automatic a choice as possible? The goal is to increase engagement to get the energy flowing in a way that's useful and creative and moves you forward. When the energy is right, you are better able to attend to both aspects of engaging with others—the result you want from the interaction and the relationship itself.

(Bob) Imagine that you and I are having a conversation. I can't control what's going on in your mind, but I do have some control over what's going on in my mind. Even if we're talking in a soundproofed, white-walled room, there will always be potential distractions—random thoughts, concerns from elsewhere in my life, worries about the errands I have to run later today. There's always a certain amount of internal chatter. Still, I do have the opportunity to make the choice to be or not to be engaged.

> If I let my mind wander, then I've lost connection with you and with what we're talking about. I'm gone, focused on something else. I've disrupted the energy flow between us, and we're probably not going to get the result we were looking for. In addition, I may affect our relationship by causing you to experience an ARGUE response—for example, you may feel angry ("This jerk is not listening to me!") or unworthy ("I'm so boring, no one ever listens to me").

For parents, managers, and other leaders, this kind of modeling can be extremely important. In many situations, you have to do more than just *be* engaged. You also have to make sure that the other person *knows* you're engaged. Of course, not everybody engages in the same way. People who are aural learners will listen better if they close their eyes. People who are kinesthetic learners may have to do something like take notes. You not only need to engage with others, you also need to understand how others like to have you engage with them.

Engagement and Multitasking

With the onslaught of technological innovation—BlackBerries, iPods, chat rooms, and even cellphones—the concept and practice of multitasking has become an even bigger part of our lives. If your objective is to ensure that the energy is flowing, and you find that you really need to be fully engaged, does that mean that you can't multitask?

We believe that you can multitask, as long as all the tasks are focused on the same *result* and the same set of *relationships*. Imagine that you're in a meeting and you're taking notes. You may not be looking the speaker in the eye, and yet you're fully engaged. Your note-taking is helping you listen to, understand, and recall what other people are saying. At the same time, it's triggering other ideas you may want to explore, which benefits both you and those who depend on you. That's high engagement both in the result and in the relationship.

> *(Bob)* One of my clients is an executive who operates a virtual company with 50 staff. He works from home four days a week, and the way he manages the company from his home office is a really remarkable example of multitasking engagement.
>
> He has set up his computer with three screens. He uses a headset. Let's watch him in action:
>
> • When he gets a call from a customer, he stays engaged with the customer on the phone, asking questions about the person's situation and listening closely.
> • At the same time, he quickly instant-messages his operations manager and says, "I've got so-and-so on the phone; what's going on with this installation?"
> • He also looks at his contact database to see who's been in there last, which consultants have been working there, and what's been going on with the installation.
> • At the same time he also has access to a record of emails summarizing everything that's been going on with this case. He has every possible bit of information available.
>
> This versatile and dexterous fellow is highly engaged, and his activities are all focused on the same result and the same set of relationships.

Contrast this example with that of a 13-year-old friend of the family who recently told me, "My brain is so fast I can definitely multitask."

I observed her for a while as she did her homework accessing the Internet. She had rock music playing, which didn't exactly fade into the background. At the same time, she had an Internet chat going with one friend as she talked on her headset phone with another friend.

She seemed to be managing all these channels at once, and it seemed to me that every one of those channels got short shrift. More than a few times I heard her say, "What was that again?"

In the context of the first of those two examples, multitasking is very powerful. But the communication shortcuts that technology provides can also provide opportunities for disengagement— sometimes notoriously so as in the case of the reckless driver who pays too much attention to his cellphone conversation. The more of these technologies you have in your lives, the more you need to stay mindfully aware of your degree of engagement.

(*Julia*) I observed an exchange at a restaurant recently. It was pretty typical, though it struck me as really interesting anyway.

Two men were eating and talking at a table adjacent to ours. A cellphone rang. One of them stopped talking, checked the phone to see who was calling, and put his phone to his ear. He said (more loudly than necessary, which seems to be a common phenomenon), "Listen, I'm at lunch so I can't speak with you right now. Can I call you back later?"

In less than one minute, this man managed to disengage himself from both his lunch partner (by cutting off their conversation to deal with the phone) *and* the caller (because of the dismissive bluntness of his exchange). He could have avoided the whole thing in the first place by simply turning off his cellphone.

That's why it's becoming a matter of contemporary etiquette to have people turn their cellphones and BlackBerries off in group meetings. You probably don't need to be in touch unless you've got a really special situation.

In the current cultural and technological climate, you're vulnerable to being disengaged and to having your energy flow disrupted. When technology is easy to use, people will use it, without necessarily thinking about the consequences. In the end, though, it's your choice whether and when you need or want to be reached. Part of staying mindfully aware is understanding the impact these choices can have on your energy flow, and making a choice about how you want to use technology to support your desired outcomes. It's the difference between actively engaging the technology and being enslaved by the technology.

Great leaders are masters of engagement. According to Jim Collins, author of the book *Good to Great*, the most effective leaders are highly engaged, and one of the things they do better than anyone else is to listen. And this is not just about business. Think of the people in your personal life who have meant so much to you. They probably were, and are, people who get and stay highly personally engaged with you as an individual.

Engagement is all about making choices and making them by staying mindfully aware of those choices. In the next two chapters, we'll look deeper into the vowel of engagement in order to understand how your choices can become more effective. We'll first look at how you can use the practice of *staying resolved without attachment*. Then we'll delve into the practice of *supportive mutuality*. Both of these will require you to engage with others more openly to achieve your own objectives.

6

Stay Resolved Without Attachment

It may sound like a contradiction to talk about staying *resolved* without being *attached*. What do we mean by these terms?

Whereas being resolved means having a clear and useful vision of what you mean to achieve, being attached means you have too much of our own identity invested in something—for example, a belief or a way of doing things or just a feeling of possession of the idea you're resolved to making a reality. This kind of attachment has the potential of making you behave differently from the way you might behave if you had only resolve. Let's look at an example.

> *(Julia)* I grew up in a family without much money. My parents taught me that if I wanted something, it was better to wait until I could pay for it. That meant I had to save my allowance to get things that I "wanted" (in contrast to things I needed, which my parents bought). It's easy to imagine that I didn't end up getting a lot of things I wanted, since my allowance was not big and it took me a long time to save up for the things my

friends were getting from their parents.

When I began to earn my own money, I learned that it was important to establish a credit rating in order to eventually be able to buy a car or a house. I knew that paying cash for things would not help me do this. Being able to afford something began to mean something other than having the cash to pay for it—it meant using my credit card and paying it off before the date it was due. Using this new approach, I learned to live with managed debt. As a result of accepting this new way of thinking about how I could afford things, my life has taken a very different route.

If I had thought of the world as being a world of scarcity, which was certainly my perception and reality in childhood, I would have behaved very differently. And if I had formed this association at a young age (my cash allowance isn't very big, therefore I can't afford very much), it is likely that I would have stayed attached to that position, even though it may not always have helped me achieve my goals.

Because I was able to stay resolved to the notion of being able to afford something without being attached to the idea of paying cash for everything, my life changed for the better.

Staying Resolved with Your Thoughtful I

Staying resolved is important when you're trying to achieve a goal. It means looking at the longer-term outcome and staying mindfully aware of the attachments you may have formed that may get in your way, while still living life in the present moment. It's important to recognize this because you can act only in the present. You cannot change the past and you have only potential influence on the future. And that influence will be a direct product of how you act in the present.

> *(Julia)* A good metaphor to use for looking at these issues of resolve and attachment is the CEO. Consider this and replace the word "CEO" with parent, teacher, or community leader.
>
> The most effective CEOs I know have a positive vision of what their company is going to do and are always talking about the vision and acting in support of it. It's certainly not all about them. These people are definitely interested in getting others engaged. And they demonstrate their willingness to allow other people to give nuance to the approaches that are going to achieve the vision. This kind of leader drives the organization forward, staying resolved in the pursuit of the vision and unattached to any particular way of achieving it.

You may be asking yourself how you can stay resolved at the level of intent and purpose, yet avoid becoming too attached to specific ways of doing things.

Many Successful Ways to a Common End

Staying resolved without attachment depends on accepting and supporting mutuality, which is the focus of the next chapter. We'll just touch on the notion here.

> *(Julia)* Let's go back to the CEOs. What becomes obvious is that the people in the organizations with an effective CEO become committed to the vision. They know they will be more successful themselves if they help the CEO move toward the

vision. As they become resolved, and begin to share ideas, it becomes easier for everyone to let go of any attachments they may have had. The result is that the best ideas are incorporated into the implementation of the vision, and everyone wins. The value of supportive mutuality becomes obvious.

When it comes to being in business, being a parent, or being a teacher, you have many connections that you depend on for success. If you want to achieve a particular outcome, you must realize that although you may think you know the best way to get there, your idea represents only one of many that are possible. The best thing to do is to stay resolved to the outcome and remain unattached to the way you think it should be pursued. By being open to the ideas and influences of other people and their different perspectives, you may discover a different and more effective way to achieve success.

(Bob) The writing of this book has been a real education for me.

I started it three times in the last four years and found myself ending the project after the first couple of chapters each time. I first took the approach of following a case history with one of my consulting clients and running it through all the practices. That ended after chapter 2 when my brother said to me, after I pestered him to give me some feedback, "You are going to hire a professional writer, aren't you?"

The second try was a straight description of the practices. Boring. Stopped that after the first pass.

Effort number three was having a marketing consultant with a background in TV journalism help us write up a story. While that did help us understand and refine the model, it didn't fly as a book.

Julia and I then took over a year to nail down the content of each practice and describe each one in two to three pages. As we developed the practices, we sent them out by email to business colleagues and personal friends to get their feedback.

Finally, with all that material in hand, we turned to a professional editor who took our system along with many hours of taped interviews and worked with us intensively to produce what you're reading now.

There were several points along that path where I felt like packing it in. However, I felt so strongly about getting these messages out to the world, I was able to stay resolved to the end. "Keep the end in mind," as Stephen Covey puts it. And with that, I gained increasing comfort with turning to others to help shape how that end would be achieved.

If you are attached not just to an outcome but to *a way of getting to the outcome*, you are putting that outcome in danger of never being reached. Why? Because you have not leveraged the ideas and energy of other people. "No man is an island," as the saying goes.

Engaging the Energy of Others Makes Life Easier

Getting others involved in determining how to get to a desired end gets their energy flowing and increases their commitment to that end as they now have some "skin in the game."

(*Julia*) I'm always fascinated when staying resolved to an outcome coupled with the lack of attachment to the "how" makes it easier for other people to become engaged with someone else's outcome. People are much more likely to share ideas with someone who is committed to a concept without being adamant about how to implement it than with someone who has a "my way or the highway" approach. It's so much easier to engage with committed and flexible people.

In my experience as a manager, I found that if I got too attached to a fixed way of doing things, I was too controlling to be a good boss. I would end up depleting people's energy as they tried to do things their way and I caught them at it instead of waiting for the results. I could see them becoming actively disengaged from the outcome, and committed only to getting the job done the way I wanted it.

The problem was that their grudging acquiescence then affected my own energy. The outcome—if we even got it—was never as meaningful as when we were able to really work together toward a jointly owned outcome—collaboratively.

So I learned the lesson the hard way. What a transformation when I stayed resolved about the outcome and let go of my attachment to my way of doing things! The people who worked for me came up with ideas I would never have thought of. Some of those ideas worked better than others, and some of them didn't work at all. Yet when I stayed resolved to a jointly owned outcome and let my team figure out how to get there, their energy was high, and they were always willing to go the extra mile to get the job done. They truly stayed resolved.

The same is true in families. Just try inviting your spouse or children to collaborate on decisions, instead of barking orders at them, and you'll see remarkable results.

We believe that everyone has something to offer and wants to offer that something in order to enjoy a sense of belonging and contributing. What you can do for them is demonstrate your resolve with respect to the outcome and your willingness to hear their ideas regarding how to achieve it. By not becoming attached to one particular way of doing things, you liberate people's creative energy. You liberate them to use whatever talents they have in order to achieve the desired outcome—even a difficult one.

> *(Bob)* Chris, a friend of mine, attends a church where the congregation and leadership have a lot of heart, passion, caring, and commitment, but it's also a church that is getting older. People are talking about wanting to help the church grow, and seem to expect the senior leadership to come up with a strategy for growth. Chris feels, however, that those at the level of senior leadership aren't sure of the vision or ultimate outcome of their church anymore.
>
> Chris, who leads the church choir, can see the confusion at the leadership level and has chosen not be a part of that bigger discussion, but to demonstrate, through his methods of leading the choir, how he believes the leadership could best proceed toward their vision for the church as a whole. He knows that his talents are best used at the level he's comfortable with—music.
>
> He knows he can keep the choir going at a high level, and hold out for the cavalry to come in with some better leadership. He's basically saying to the leadership, "While you're busy sorting yourselves out, I'll keep this aspect going strong. That will be my contribution to the larger goal." This is his way of doing things. He understands and is engaged with the larger vision for the church, and knows that by leading the choir toward success like this, his achievements and enthusiasm will spread to other parts of the church.

This illustrates the valuable lesson that you need to understand how and where you can best contribute. You need to know your own talents and abilities, and you also need to know where to use them, whether in your work environment or that of your family and community.

To achieve a goal, however modest or grand it may be, you need to stay resolved. This means having a vision that is clear and unwavering, and letting that vision guide you as you move toward your goal. Getting or staying attached to a particular way of getting there can halt the journey entirely, however. It can discourage the people you depend on to help you reach your goal and it can block the energy flow you need to find ways to get there. Letting go of your attachments gives you the kind of flexibility that works best with your resolve so that you can move steadily and effectively toward your vision.

7

Accept — and Support — Your Mutuality

As human beings, we are not isolated islands. While it may be possible for some, it's extremely unusual for anyone to live entirely alone, dependent on no one. Most of us have at least one other person in our lives and usually a good many more. In general, we are interdependent with countless others, day in and day out, in more ways than it's possible to realize.

We depend an enormous amount on the pilot of the plane to know his or her job and be able to take off, get us to our destination in one piece, and land us safely. We trust every day, on the roads and highways, that the person coming toward us knows how to drive and is healthy and stable enough right now to keep their car in their lane. Most of us depend every day on vast networks of individuals who teach our children, manage our money, grow or prepare the food products we eat, and on and on it goes. Even so, much of the time we're not doing a stellar job of depending and trusting that others are going to do what we need them to do.

Your task now is to take engagement to a deeper level—from

"I'm engaging with you in this moment" to "I'm dependent on you and you're dependent on me for real success."

In The Energy Exchange, we call this interdependence "supportive mutuality." You will find that when you approach others with this notion in mind, it is much easier for your energy to flow and for you to get the results you want.

Supportive Mutuality Is an Attitude

(Julia) A memory from my years at university illustrates the notion of supportive mutuality really well, and deals with the reservation people may have about its being calculating and manipulative.

One of my best friends and I were going to the registrar's office to get some advice about some exam schedule conflicts we had. There was a long line-up and we didn't have a lot of time—we had left it too late, of course.

We were both starting to ARGUE. Specifically, we were angry and resentful about the number of other people who were in line, and feeling guilty that we had left the problem unresolved for so long. And then I remembered something that my mother had told me once: "If you treat people with respect and courtesy, they will do the same for you. And if they don't, you haven't lost anything but some time."

I told Val to stay in the big line while I tried something else. I went up to another wicket where there was no line and approached the young man behind the counter with a smile (I must have been mindfully aware of my need to counter the thundercloud that had been hovering over my head). I explained that while I knew he was not involved in fixing scheduling problems (the sign above the wicket told me that), I figured that he knew what some of the rules were. I told the fellow (he was a student doing this as a part-time job) what our problem was and asked him how we could expedite resolving our issue.

He told me we would need specific documentation to get an alternative exam date, and that we needed to get it before we got into the long line. I thanked him, asked for his name, and told him I would put a note into the registrar's office about how helpful he had been. He had saved us a lot of time and aggravation. If we had got to the front of the line and been turned away—well, I shudder to think what would have happened.

We came back early the next morning with the documentation we needed, and it turned out that the young man I had dealt with the day before was now handling exam conflicts. We were done in a flash, getting the resolution we had been hoping for. I handed him the note I had written to the registrar and told him I would write another one telling the end of the story. He laughed and told us to have a good day.

Accepting and supporting mutuality allows the energy to flow between you and those around you. It sets you up to work with others and not against them; it sets you up to look at the possibilities instead of the obstacles in front of you. This open attitude encourages others to reciprocate in kind, and the energy flows easily. Taking a position of supportive mutuality also means that you're likely have a smile on your face more often than not when you start a dialogue with another person. And a smile, as we all know, is powerfully contagious.

Mutuality is a condition you can wrestle with or welcome. Consider:

- When you fail to understand and accept your interdependence with others, you end up wrestling with them instead of collaborating productively.
- When you allow your fears about the motives or limitations of others to hijack you, you block the energy flow and reduce everyone's chances of being successful.
- When you welcome others' input, you benefit from their wisdom and their resources and you multiply your own possibilities for success. The energy flows in all directions and everyone wins.

Supportive Mutuality Is Contagious

Mutuality begets mutuality. You may start out embracing interdependence in order to reap the benefits in improved relationships and mutual success and before long find that mutuality just feels good in its own right.

> *(Bob)* Recently I was considering hiring a designer to help rework my personal website. I arranged a meeting with one potential contractor through a friend. As I went into my first meeting with him, I had no idea whether he was going to be the right person for the job, or whether I even wanted to hire someone.
>
> Mindfully aware that this meeting could be seen as merely a fishing expedition on my part, I flipped the switch on supportive mutuality, remembering to look for ways I could contribute to his success.

I told him about my position, being thoughtfully authentic as I did so. "I don't know where I'm going with this project or who's going to do it," I said. "I may still end up doing the work myself, but I'd love to talk to you about design."

In the end, by telling him about my goals and then by showing and eventually sending him my graphics and ideas, I allowed him to use this exchange as an opportunity for his own success. By using my materials as a springboard for his own design ideas, he was able to come up with a great design that meant success for us both. Flipping the switch was a critical step.

Supportive Mutuality Makes Marriage Easier

Often we decide fairly smoothly, with many of the people in our lives, when and how to embrace mutuality. And with our loved ones? Not so much. In our families we're involved every day in interdependencies of extraordinary subtlety and importance, and we usually don't have the luxury of choosing the time and place. This means we have to always stay mindfully aware of what success means to those close to us, and to always be thinking about how we can help them achieve that success.

(Julia) A friend of mine told me a story about a newly married couple. The young man had gone into engineering because that's what his parents had wanted him to do. He had graduated after four years and got a job in a small engineering firm. The young woman had pursued a liberal arts degree and had been successful in joining a large corporation in sales. They met when she made a sales call on the engineering firm. They

started seeing each other shortly after that.

Not too long after they began dating, the young man told his girlfriend that he had quit his job. He told her he had been miserable all through engineering school and could not look forward to devoting his life to a career that would make him miserable. He wanted to go back to school and get a master's degree in English, so he could become a teacher. He also told her that he wanted to ask her to be his wife, but felt he could not do so under the circumstances.

Now this young woman was wise beyond her years. Instead of ARGUEing, she told the young man first that she would marry him, and second that she would support him in going back to school, if that's what was going to make him happy. She told him she wanted to be able to stay home with their children, when they finally had them, and knew he would support her in that.

She clearly understood that their success as a married couple depended on each of them being supportive of the other. And I believe he did, too. They're still married, and have two lovely children. He teaches English, and she has her own company, which she started from her home when the kids were both in school.

Supportive Mutuality Works with Kids, Too

It becomes more difficult for you to engage in supportive mutuality when a family member does something you don't like or understand. Parents whose children exercise their individuality through their appearance, for example, will often feel as if this reflects badly on them and their parenting skills. Parents who tell you they have brought their children up to be independent, coura-geous, and willing to stand up for what they believe in make a big exception when their children tell them they have a right to wear what they want wherever they want.

How does supportive mutuality work in this kind of situation? With the parents staying mindfully aware of what is important to the children and being thoughtfully authentic in telling the chil-dren what is important to them. This means acknowledging that the statement they are making with their clothing or haircut is valid and is important to them. It also means explaining that, as parents, your own wish for them to dress respectably and respectfully is equally valid and important.

As a parent, you need to model behavior that clearly is *not* "all about me," in order to demonstrate that you understand that your children's needs are just as valid as your own. You also need to cher-ish your lightness, remembering not to take yourself too seriously. At the same time, you have to take your children's attempts to estab-lish themselves as people seriously—after all, that's what most parents want for them.

Families who engage in this type of dialogue will succeed in find-ing an answer that satisfies everyone's definition of success and will leave the loving relationship intact.

Is it easy to do? It certainly takes time and effort. And the expen-diture of both is worth the effort, considering the potential results —and the negative results that are likely when parents try a power play in this area.

> *(Bob)* My relationship with my daughter is an ongoing example of the importance of staying mindfully aware of and support-ing mutuality. When I look at Rome, I think of what I can do to

help her be successful and how that translates into being a good parent, which is part of my definition of success.

Through dialogue, Dorothy and I can come to a sense of what success is for Rome. The job falls to us as parents because as a young child, Rome, is not able to understand or articulate what success means for her. That's continuing to evolve.

One of the elements of her success, we think, is not being afraid to try new things, while at the same time having a strong sense of what it means to take prudent risks. We believe it's important for her to look at the positive side of things and not become overly bound by rules and negativity.

Let me illustrate what this means.

It so happens that Rome loves climbing trees. My responses could be:

- "Rome, you're not allowed to climb trees. It's dangerous."
- Or "Climb the tree, but don't fall."
- Or "Don't climb too high or you'll fall and break a leg."

So there we were, walking the dogs in the park and swimming into our view came a tree that was just made for climbing. For Rome, success meant climbing that tree. For me, success meant that she climbed the tree in such a way as to stay safe and get down by herself without falling. The challenge for me was to teach a five-year-old what a calculated risk was when she was wanting to climb halfway up a tree that was 40 feet tall.

As she started up the tree, I looked at the possible paths she could take, assessing their ability to carry Rome's weight. I also stood in a position where I could break her fall should she lose her balance.

As she approached one dead branch, I asked her how she might test whether the branch could hold her. She figured it out and said, "If I hold onto this one above, I can step on this branch and see if it's strong enough."

With that, the next time she came to a questionable branch, she asked me about it. We were developing a dialogue that would allow each of us to achieve what we wanted.

Supportive Mutuality Is a Conscious Choice

To ensure supportive mutuality, you need to stay mindfully aware of what success means to you in any given situation. There are times when you are interacting with others and you're not looking for any real outcome. What do you do about supportive mutuality in those cases?

It's important to think about your own big picture, about how you define success for yourself. It's also important for you to ensure that the energy you put into our day-to-day encounters with others is fueled by that definition of success. And while this book is not about how to develop such a definition, we believe that using the notion of supportive mutuality in your relationships with family, friends, and colleagues will help you do so as you make the conscious choice to use this practice.

(Julia) I'm attempting to help build my son Jess's competence in his own ever-changing world. And yet I have a personal need to mother him and nurture him. We have a standing joke. If I say to him, "Would you like cookies and milk?" he says, "Ma, if I wanted cookies and milk I could get it myself. But since you want to take care of me, how about four cook-

ies and a really big glass of milk?"

And then he lets me get the snack for him because he understands that my definition of success is maintaining the nurturing connection with him, even as I recognize the requirement for me to accept that he's able to take care of himself.

Whether you're dealing with a co-worker, employee, child, or the clerk at the end of a long line, accepting and supporting your mutuality will help both of you get what you need.

Making Engagement Work for You

The two of us take quite different approaches to implementing the three practices of engagement.

(Julia) With all of the roles I play in my life, it's often been difficult for me to get and stay engaged. So it has been critical for me to stay mindfully aware that the present is called the present because it is a gift. The hard work I have to do to stay engaged in the moment is made a lot easier with the notion of accepting and supporting my mutuality with others. My Thoughtful I reminds me that it's not all about me, that it's not all about what I have to do or about the way I want to do it. It's about both or all of us getting the results we want in the most creative and productive way possible.

One of the things I have found helps me manage my awareness is the habit of thankfulness. At this point, I don't know whether awareness or thankfulness comes first. What I do know is that being more aware, and being more thankful, allows my energy to flow more easily and allows me to step more lightly in this complex world of ours.

(Bob) To me, engagement is all about being in the present moment. It's my choice to either tune in or tune out. Life is happening where I tune in.

And where do I tune in? Into the task I am doing at the time? A conversation I am in? Is the buzz of the BlackBerry or cellphone beckoning me to a new conversation? The choice I make has an impact both on those around me and on who I will become.

Engaging in the present moment—as the point of power—allows me to create that preferred future I covet. As I hold tightly to the vision of the end I am creating and allow the universe to show me the best way to get there, my engagement moves me surely to the end in mind.

That's where my mutuality with others comes in. For me, accepting and supporting my mutuality with others is a going-in position rather than a result. When I am about to go into a conversation with people I have not met before—whether in a personal or a professional setting—I turn on a mental switch that keeps me thinking, "The people I'm meeting and I are interdependent; I can help them be successful and they, in turn, can affect my success."

So how do you begin adopting these three practices to enhance your level of engagement in what's going on around you?

Start by checking in with yourself every so often and asking the simple questions:

- Am I engaged?
- How do I know?

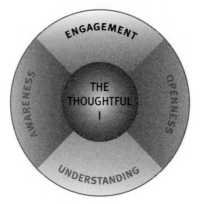

Then, if you're not satisfied with the answers, think about which of the three practices would be most useful to you in enhancing your engagement.

OPENNESS

The Thoughtful I and Openness

By the time most of us reach the point of raising our own families, we have established patterns of how we believe we should live. The shoulds and shouldn'ts are firmly entrenched, and we have strong opinions—expressed or not—regarding how things should be done. We are by now far less open to new ways of doing things than when we entered this world.

To be able to live the rich and full life you were meant for means opening yourself up to continually considering new ways of doing things, while preserving the core of what still works for you. In business we call it "continuous improvement," and, in more significant change initiatives, "reengineering."

What's good for the goose—business and enterprise—is good for the gander—ourselves.

Whatever the situation or context, you need to engage your Thoughtful I. When you continue with automatic thought, your responses to different ideas are going to be the familiar, "That's not the way we do it here," and "That wouldn't work in our family," and "If it was good enough for my parents, it's good enough for me."

By activating your Thoughtful I, you can wrest those automatic statements out of your throat before they do any damage. You can change your thoughts about the different approaches that are being presented and become much more open to the amazing possibilities that lie ahead of you.

This section, on the vowel of openness, deals with these three practices:

- Accept Every Idea's Inevitable Relevance
- Allow—and Fully Appreciate—Fresh Associations
- Perceive the Positives

8

Accept Every Idea's Inevitable Relevance

The three practices in this section help you stay open to ideas. This first chapter in the trio is about getting yourself into a frame of mind that allows you to begin the process of becoming open to new ways of looking at things. Like supportive mutuality, it can take the form of flipping on a mental switch just to avoid premature dismissal of any idea.

Validation of Ideas = Validation of People

Accepting every idea's inevitable relevance is akin to the ancient parable of sowing seed that falls on different types of soil. If you immediately reject an idea, that idea, like seed cast on the rocky ground, has no chance of manifesting itself and making a contribution. If instead, you value an idea and allow it to be heard, whether it is immediately applicable or not, you are sowing the idea in soil where it has at least a fighting chance to take root and survive. It may gestate and grow strong and really make a difference.

The beauty of this is that when you consciously and verbally accept the inevitable relevance of an idea, you transmit unconditional acceptance of the individual who broached it. You thus "validate" the individual—and this is true even if you're just considering an idea in and of yourself.

In a group setting, this practice tells other people in the conversation that it's OK to come up with ideas.

If you dismiss an idea—even with a simple "no"—you can cause the other person to withdraw from the conversation or fully disengage. Your dismissal may actively sabotage further dialogue.

What About Half-baked Ideas?

The notion of accepting every idea's relevance makes some people nervous. "What if you affirm a half-baked idea and it leads to something really embarrassing or terrible?" they wonder. Our answer to that is that in the end, you really don't need to "deselect" an idea when it's presented. If it really cannot be made applicable to the matter at hand, it will not be chosen in the final decision process. Or, in some almost Darwinian fashion, it will not survive. Yet, it remains in the knowledge pool and is therefore available to others to see its relevance in other situations.

To keep track of these ideas for future reference, you can record them in the "not yet" column or the "pool of potential relevance." At some point, some of those ideas will be categorized as "an idea whose time has come."

Inevitable Relevance and Energy Flow

Judging that an idea is *not* relevant blocks energy within us and between us. Allowing an idea to survive liberates energy.

> *(Bob)* I think there's an interesting twist to the phrase, "For a kid with a new hammer, everything looks like a nail."
>
> The intent of the statement is to belittle the individual who tries to apply his new pet theory to everything in sight or earshot.
>
> On the other side of this, if we approach this with a mindset of exploration and experimentation, we may just find a different and productive use for our new "hammer."
>
> We just have to ensure we don't take ourselves too seriously.

When you don't feel good about a certain situation or idea, it means your thoughts are focused on what's wrong or what's missing. When you think negative thoughts, negative emotions are bound to follow, and your energy flow is affected.

When you accept every idea's inevitable relevance, you allow the idea a chance to survive, while addressing any issues you may have with it. In doing so, you do not block the energy of the person whose idea it was, nor do you block the creativity of others who may have other ideas or ways to address the issues you have identified. Even if you end up using a completely different idea from the original one, you will all be mindfully aware that you would not have succeeded in coming up with the solution had it not been for the original idea. And the original idea may well find a use in another situation.

Focusing on Thoughts, Not Emotions

There are times when you will be tempted to discard an idea as irrelevant because of your feelings about the person presenting the idea. Perhaps you feel the person does not understand the situation, or has a set of values so different from yours that their insights can't possibly be relevant to you. Invoking the Thoughtful I when using this practice can help you focus on the idea separately from the person who has offered it.

> *(Bob)* Several years ago, up at our family cottage at the end of the summer, members of my extended family and I were having dinner. I mentioned that I would be closing up the cottage in a few weeks—which, at that time, I always did on my own.
>
> My young nephew piped up that he would be glad to stay and help me.
>
> I thought I had better describe how much work was required, particularly in putting up the boat.
>
> "It's a lot of work to take the 90-horsepower outboard motor off and store it in the tool shed, and hoist the boat up over the slip," I said.
>
> "Why bother doing that?" he said. "Just leave it on and hoist them up together."
>
> I was about to dismiss the idea as coming from someone who was inexperienced in this work and maintained a healthy allergy to effort. Then I stopped the thought. I realized I was falling into the trap of, "It's the way we've always done it." I was about to defend my way of doing things. I remember saying, "Well, we do want to avoid having it 'grow legs' over the winter."
>
> "C'mon, Uncle Bob. That boat's 10 years old," he said. "No one's going to bother even *trying* to take it."
>
> I remember working through all the potential downsides of the idea, and finally concluding, "He's got a point."

> From then on I saved myself hours of effort by hoisting the boat up, motor and all. And he was right, the boat didn't grow legs. It was always waiting for me when I returned at the beginning of summer.

Accepting the inevitable relevance of an idea doesn't mean you have to agree with it. Doing this helps maintain your relationships and is likely to help you get a better result with whatever task is at hand.

This Practice Increases Our Possibilities

We all know that friction is necessary when we're trying to stop a car and not the least bit helpful when we're trying to slide down a snowy hill on a toboggan. It's the same with ideas. If we think about how something *might* work instead of why something *won't* work, it will help us create even more possibilities and encourage us to try new things.

That's why we recommend that you carry a notebook and pen at all times. Put a notebook on your bedside table and one in the bathroom. Whenever an interesting thought comes to you—even one with no apparent application in the present—write it down. When you find your energy blocked regarding an idea or a situation, consulting your ideas book may just give you the inspiration you need to move forward.

A great statement is, "This year's exam is the same as last year's exam—it's just the answers that are different." The right answer to the same question can change over time. Likewise, a certain concept, idea, or approach may be more useful at one point in time than at another.

Consider a number of wartime leaders—George Patton, Dwight Eisenhower, Winston Churchill—who are accepted as having made a significant difference in victory by the Allies in World War II. Their records as peacetime leaders were not nearly as memorable. That does not, however, negate their effectiveness during the war. It simply means that their style may have been more appropriate in one context than in another. When that is the case for you, you need to have your Thoughtful I fully engaged so that you can stay resolved without attachment and keep your ego out of the way. It's hard work.

Mining the Sources of Ideas

A good mindset for energy flow is to see that there are ideas everywhere, coming from our colleagues and peers, from children, and, let's not forget, from *ourselves.*

> *(Bob)* I know that a lot of people overlook the wisdom of what kids say. My daughter, Rome, now nine years old, comes up with some amazing stuff.
>
> When I was talking to Dorothy about how I was designing the website for The Energy Exchange, Rome overheard and jumped into the conversation, saying, "Can I help you, Daddy? I've got some great ideas for the site."
>
> "Sure, Rome," I said.
>
> "For example, on the page we'll use for the Power of the Both-Handed, we could …"
>
> "Rome, that's brilliant!" I said. "I had never thought of it that way—both-handed captures it beautifully."
>
> Without missing a beat, she said, "And we could put a picture of two hands on the page, one with something nice in it, and

the other with something else nice, and ..."

After the incident, I realized that the conversation could have gone at least three different ways, depending on my **beliefs** and my **thoughts** about her comment at the time. Here's what I observed:

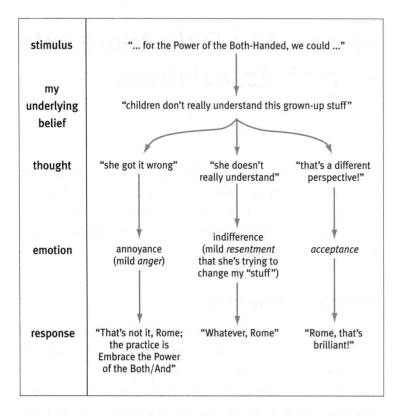

stimulus	"... for the Power of the Both-Handed, we could ..."		
my underlying belief	"children don't really understand this grown-up stuff"		
thought	"she got it wrong"	"she doesn't really understand"	"that's a different perspective!"
emotion	annoyance (mild *anger*)	indifference (mild *resentment* that she's trying to change my "stuff")	*acceptance*
response	"That's not it, Rome; the practice is Embrace the Power of the Both/And"	"Whatever, Rome"	"Rome, that's brilliant!"

If I had pursued either of the first two paths, I would have thwarted her energy, not only losing a great creative contribution but also stifling her creative thinking, especially if I continued to use that type of response in other situations.

9

Allow—and Fully Appreciate —Fresh Associations

Cooks use fresh associations all the time. They are open to trying new spices, new cheeses, new combinations of ingredients, new cooking methods. They may, however, be the exceptions. From early in life, most of us get locked into very particular ways of seeing things. How does this happen?

Getting Stuck in Our Truths

As discussed above, by the age of three or four, the average child has absorbed a universe of *shoulds* and *shouldn'ts*, *goods* and *bads*. These habits and beliefs form the relatively rigid framework within which each of us functions for the rest of our lives—guiding us in how to behave and how to react to the actions of other people. They form the core of our own truths.

We learn some of these patterns for ourselves because they work for us. For example, I have the habit of keeping my wallet in my back pocket. This has worked for me for years because it's accessible back there and I don't have to fish around for it. There may be other ways of carrying it, but I stick with this way because it hasn't failed me yet.

Other "truths" are imposed by the influential people in our lives, including parents, grandparents, friends, siblings, teachers, daycare supervisors, and police officers. Your mother may have told you, early on, that you should read the newspaper every day to keep track of the world around you. Now, even though there are lots of other media outlets available, and even though your lifestyle may have changed since she gave you the advice, you may still feel a sense of duty to read the paper every day.

These diehard habits you form, whether they serve you well or not, can distract you from the alternatives and keep you from making fresh associations.

(Bob) I like to prepare roast chicken up at the cottage. I was never very enthusiastic, though, about cleaning the oven, which is not a self-cleaning one.

One day I thought of treating the barbecue outside the cottage as an oven, rather than just a grill. I brought the barbecue temperature up to high, placed the chicken in an aluminum foil roasting pan and placed it on the grill, then turned the heat down to medium-low. As it cooked, I basted the chicken in its own juices, and after an hour it was done.

The resulting chicken was moist throughout, and tasted better to me than when I used a rotisserie or a standard oven. And certainly there wasn't as much cleaning to do. Little things can transform a lot of what you do.

> *(Julia)* I struggled for many years trying to grow grass in my backyard. It doesn't get a lot of sun, and the trees are old so the roots make it difficult to plant anything there. I asked an 80-year-old retired gardener what I could do to solve my problem and he sounded like David Letterman, saying, "Two words: bark nuggets." Now I don't have any grass back there at all, just bark nuggets eight inches deep. People are so hung up on the idea of having the perfect lawn, and the truth is there are a lot of other things you can do with your yard. Oh, and many of the ideas save on water and eliminate the need for pesticides.

When you do have a new idea, you sometimes scold yourself, saying, "Why didn't I think of that before?" Nearly everyone has been frustrated with an uncooperative appliance, trying complicated maneuvers to get it to work, only to discover that you simply forgot to plug it in. It can come as quite a surprise, when you do allow for a fresh association, that you could have been so blind or so stubborn before.

Cut yourself some slack. We love the story about an Icelandic woman who opened a museum near Reykjavik when she was 94 years old. "Why did you wait until you were 94 to open a museum?" a reporter asked her. "I didn't think of it before," she serenely replied.

A Simple Idea Can Be More Effective Than a Sophisticated One

A business colleague of ours used to say that the reason he was so successful was that he was lazy. He didn't want to put out the effort, so he'd figure out how to do something the simplest possible way.

People like our friend think of complex ideas as rather useless.

Others of us may be attracted to complexity and overlook simpler ideas, in doing so missing lots of opportunities.

> *(Bob)* My wife and I planned to visit friends out of town. The way our schedules were arranged had us leaving the city at rush hour. We knew there would be terrible traffic, so we spent hours trying to map out the most efficient route. We studied our maps and used different Internet-based mapping programs and agonized over the logistics of a very complicated route.
>
> And so it was that we set out on our trip. The traffic turned out to be the worst we had ever experienced. As we sat in gridlock, it dawned on us that the best solution would have been the simplest one: take the train and avoid the whole planning and traffic ordeal entirely.

Sometimes it helps to keep asking questions until you've made the situation simple. Even if you think you've arrived at a solution, it can be useful to take another pass at it and make sure you're not overlooking an obvious—and possibly superior—answer.

> *(Julia)* My friend Marlena was organizing a wedding shower for her sister. Right from the outset, she ran into trouble scheduling it. Because the wedding was going to be in the summer, it seemed that no matter what date she picked for the shower, someone was going to be on vacation during that time. Marlena was tying herself up in knots. She was wondering whether she'd have to plan two or even three separate showers, or whether she'd have to figure out whom to exclude. Then it occurred to her to slow down and reassess the situation.
>
> So she started asking herself questions: Does my sister want

a proper shower, or is it more important to her that all her friends can be present? Does the shower need to be elaborate and follow the usual rules? Does it even need to happen at the conventional time?

Marlena soon realized that the situation was actually a lot simpler than she had thought. Her sister was an unconventional person and cared more about her friends than about tradition or etiquette.

So she planned the shower for April, before anyone's summer vacation would begin—and three months before the date of the wedding. Sure, the timing was unusual, but the scheduling worked perfectly and the event was just what the bride wanted.

Peripheral Vision Stimulates Associations

One way to allow new associations to occur is to keep an eye out for potential solutions to all the little problems or frustrations on your mind. It's like being aware of what's happening down the side streets as you walk along Main Street.

(Bob) A few years ago, four of us were playing Scrabble on the coffee table in our cottage living room. After each of us took our turn, we had to turn the board so the next player could see the board the right way up. In the process, tiles kept getting knocked from their places.

As one of us was concentrating on her next word, she spied the Lazy Susan turntable in the dining room adjacent. She quickly made the association that we could put the Scrabble board on the turntable and rotate it without jostling the tiles. It worked beautifully.

Opposites Can Work Together

It can be useful to look at opposites and see how they may actually work together. Two ideas may seem to be in opposition and turn out to be set up this way in our minds only because we can't see how they're both right.

> *(Julia)* When my family was deciding where to go on vacation one March break, I decided that my preference was to go skiing in Whistler instead of having a beach holiday in Florida. The two aren't opposites and I don't prefer one activity over the other—in fact, I enjoy them equally. However, it was convenient to see them in opposition to each other because I was anxious at the time about our family budget.
>
> However, once I realized why I was setting the two ideas in opposition, I was able to reconsider the whole situation. We all like Whistler, and we also like beach holidays in Florida; neither is superior to the other and we didn't have to think of it that way. Could we think of a way to do both?
>
> We started to look for a place closer to Whistler that would give us a chance to get warm and swim. Southern California seemed to be within reach, and driving there from British Columbia would give us a chance to do some wonderful sight-seeing on the way.
>
> Then we realized that there was some great skiing in California, at Mammoth Mountain. We decided to fly to California instead of driving. We would ski, and then drive the rest of the way, to San Diego. Camping on the way down to the beach would save some money, and the airline we were using allowed us to come back from a different city than the one

where we first landed.

The whole thing fell into place and we had a great vacation.

Finding Fresh Associations Together

Just as it's easier to find a solution by approaching a situation from a fresh perspective, it can be useful to look at it from the perspectives of everyone involved. If several people, with all their different perspectives, consider the problem, creative solutions may be revealed even more clearly.

(Bob) Speaking of family vacations, my family and I were hoping to go on holiday in France for three weeks. We were excited about the trip and were trying to figure out what to do with our two dogs. We couldn't take them with us, and we weren't comfortable leaving them in a kennel. We considered hiring a dog-sitter, until we figured out what this would cost us. It didn't seem likely that we could afford the vacation in France and the dog-sitter back at home.

Meanwhile, my niece and her boyfriend were in the midst of their own conundrum. He's a film director at the beginning of his career and was looking for a location to shoot a project. They had a tight budget and needed a very particular set—a house with a large backyard—for the film he was making. They couldn't find a location that they could afford to rent. They were running out of ideas.

The solution to each of our problems turned out to be the solution to both problems at once—and a very simple one at that. We needed a dog-sitter, they needed a location. We let them use our house (with its big backyard), and my niece agreed to look after our dogs while she was there. We didn't charge them rent and she didn't charge us a sitting fee, and all of us got what we needed.

Solutions will not always present themselves to you right away. Sometimes they need to be coaxed out, and sometimes you need to sneak up on them from behind. The practice of accepting the inevitable relevance of every idea—refusing to disregard something just because it doesn't seem, at a first glance, to lead to a solution—is part of the puzzle. Appreciating fresh associations—to allow for a surprising solution to reveal itself in an unexpected way—is another.

In the following chapter, we're going to experience the pièce de résistance of this banquet of openness—the importance and amazing results of looking for the positives in every idea.

10

Perceive the Positives

For many, being positive is difficult. From a young age, we're taught to spot the faults in things rather than the good.

> *(Bob)* When I look at the way we teach our kids, I can see that there's a tendency to focus on the negative versus the positive. For example, we mark tests out of 100. You can't get 110! With 100 as the maximum, we're always looking at something less than perfect. It's still not clear to me why we would focus so much on perfection instead of excellence.
>
> A close friend of mine used to joke about that with his kids. They would come home so proud that they got a 92%, and he'd say, "So what happened to the other 8%?" They did not regard his "joke" as particularly funny—and I know lots of other people who had the same experience with their parents.

What if you were able to turn this focus on what's missing to a focus on what's there? What if you could get your mind to spin situations in a positive way? What if you could start appreciating what's going right with life, instead of focusing on all that may be wrong with it?

In The Energy Exchange, we believe that focusing on the positive aspects of your experience will help your own energy flow. Then, once you liberate your own energy with this new way of perceiving the world, you will be able to encourage others to do the same. As is the case with each of the practices in this book, perceiving the positives will help you get rid of the blocks to your energy and allow the energy to flow, enabling you and those around you to develop and implement workable solutions.

Perceiving the Positives Is a Point of View

(Bob) When our daughter was five years old, our family traveled to Paris with an itinerary that involved a lot of stopovers. We were to fly from Toronto to Dulles Airport outside of Washington, D.C., where we had a three-hour layover before heading to London. After another three-hour layover at Heathrow Airport, we would board a flight to Paris.

I was worried because not only we were traveling with our five-year-old but with her 11-year-old cousin, as well. "What a mess," I found myself thinking. "This is going to be a nightmare, trying to keep the kids happily occupied."

My wife, looking at the same situation, said, "Wow, they're going to be so excited that they get to go into two different countries on the way to our real destination—and they'll see more airports and at least three different planes."

Dorothy was mindfully aware of all the opportunities presenting themselves, and I was looking at the itinerary as a set of problems. What a difference in the way we thought about the upcoming experience.

Her point of view enabled her to perceive the positive aspects of the trip, and her energy was contagious. She engaged the two girls in order to make the journey itself into a fun part of the vacation. As a result, the kids had a great time in the airports—shopping for bargains, taking pictures of the very different airport landscapes, counting how many languages they could hear being spoken.

In turn, their positive energy was infectious—*our* enjoyment of *their* fun made the hours go by more quickly for Dorothy and me, too. Oh, and we found a couple of great bargains!

There may be no changing the facts of a situation, but *how you view them* changes the possibilities. How and what you think about a situation influences your feelings, your behaviors, and eventually the outcome. As we say at The Energy Exchange, "Energy flows where attention goes."

If you look at a set of facts and say, "Oh, this is going to be awful," then it will be. The energy goes into making sure that the negative thing happens. It's very obedient in that sense.

How You Choose to Use Your Energy

Now, we're not saying that it's easy to see every situation positively, especially if you've been practicing looking at the problems instead of the opportunities. You've probably had times when it's been difficult getting yourself out of a negative frame of mind. It's a question of how you choose to use your energy.

(Bob) I found it fascinating to hear a long-married couple who had just come back from an Eastern European trip tell me about their experiences. They had been on a bus trip from Istanbul to Vienna over fifteen days.

The woman's eyes lit up as she talked about the history of the places they visited and the special times they had experienced. At one point, she said, they were wandering through a town and heard singing in a nearby church. They went in and found the choir practicing Handel's *Messiah* for a service later that day. They sat in a pew for two hours and enjoyed a wonderful personal concert.

As they described the trip to us, the husband every so often interjected statements concerning how the organizers of the bus tour didn't really know how to organize the tour, or how they over-charged for certain things, or how the visit to one museum was poorly arranged. It appeared that he had been determined not to enjoy it—and had succeeded.

As I like to say, "Same place, different world."

The Energy Comes from the Fourth Positive

When your brain is caught up in an analytical, critical mode of thinking—focusing overly on the negatives and the problems—it can be difficult to turn that around. Identifying the four positive aspects of a situation is one good technique for pulling yourself out of those cycles of negative thinking.

Simply ask yourself, "What are four positives to this situation or idea?" You may not know at first what the four points are, and you probably won't feel that there could even *be* four positive things.

Nonetheless, it is critical to assume there *are* four. (The truth is, there are inevitably many, many more positives than that. The task right now, however, is to identify and declare just four of them.) This exercise will help you move back into a more positive frame of mind.

Using your energy to perceive the positives can be a great advantage in problem-solving situations with friends, colleagues at work, or members of your family. This practice, when you find yourself wanting to dismiss another person's idea out of hand, or to replace it with one of your own, will help you maintain the energy flow and ensure that the best ideas to solve the problem are generated. It also helps you maintain your relationships with the people who are problem-solving with you.

> *(Julia)* At the last organization where I worked, we had an economic downturn to deal with. Business was slow, and we were brainstorming to figure out what to do to deal with the problem. I had a partner who had an amazing knack of finding the positives in almost anything that happened, and this situation was no different.
>
> While the rest of us were bemoaning the fact that we had not been out marketing for months, Adam's response was unusual.
>
> "Wait a minute," he said, "we have a great opportunity here."
>
> I could see one of my other partners poising himself to tell Adam to stop being such a Pollyanna and get down to figuring out how to get more business. Before he could interrupt him, I asked Adam what he thought the opportunity was.
>
> "Look how much more time and energy we'll have to work on other things," he said, "such as building our intellectual capital. If we take advantage of the lull in the business, then when things pick up, we'll have something to present to our clients

that will be of value to them. We may even come up with an article or two that we could publish, and that would help with our image-building and get us some 'free' publicity. Not only that, we could get some people working together who don't usually have the chance to do so, and do some team-building, too. And we could all actually close our files on engagements we have finished, something we always put off until there's more time. So you see, this quiet time is a good thing."

The rest of us were silent for a moment, and then we all began talking at once. The energy in the room had turned from negative to positive. We started making lists of the topics we wanted to explore. Adam held up his hand, and asked for everyone's attention.

"Reflecting back on our need to get business, I wish there was a way for us to get out to see all the clients we've done business with in the last two years without seeming like we're begging."

With that, another colleague in the room said, "How about asking them what kind of research they might interested in, giving us an agenda for ourselves without spending a lot of time and money, and maybe even finding out about some potential assignments?"

Did you notice how many things Adam found we could do to take advantage of the situation? And did you notice how he phrased the problem of finding out what topics were most important to our clients so we'd be sure to develop intellectual capital that had real value?

Adam found *at least four positive aspects* of the slowdown in business. And he expressed *one wish* regarding finding the solution.

Experience shows that when you've discovered the fourth

positive aspect of a situation you're in, it's as if your brain chemistry changes and it becomes easier for you to find the fifth, sixth, and even seventh positive aspects. The challenge is to stay resolved until you've managed to find the fourth positive. (After identifying three aspects, it can suddenly become difficult to think of another.) If we stick with it, the creative floodgates will open.

When Adam expressed his concern as a wish, our creative energy stayed high and we began to brainstorm ways to solve that problem. By the end of the meeting, we had a project plan that included all of Adam's ideas and many others that the rest of us had come up with. We had generated a practical way to satisfy Adam's wish, by getting out to our clients to give us feedback on their research interests.

Your energy will loosen up after you find the fourth positive. As it does so, an energy exchange will happen with the other people involved in the situation. They will begin perceiving the positives, too, and become fully engaged with you.

No matter how rough things seem to be, make yourself identify four positive aspects of the situation. It could be four positive aspects to an idea that somebody has offered, or four positive perspectives to a situation you're dealing with.

> *(Bob)* When we had the flood in our house, mentioned above, it came at an inopportune time, and both Dorothy and I were wondering how we were going to be able to handle the disruption. I work from a home office and the house was going to be largely uninhabitable for two months.
>
> One of the first things we did was sit down and say, "Well we're in this now. What can we do to take advantage of the situation?" While getting the first three positive things on the

table was difficult, the fourth was really tough.

The initial thoughts were, first, we could adjust some things we hadn't liked in the initial renovation. Second, we had experienced some minor problems with the water system before, and now we could fix it "for good." Third, we could replace some of the water-damaged furniture that we didn't really like. Then we struggled for the fourth, and finally Dorothy stated that she and our daughter could move up to our small ski cabin for six weeks—with me arriving for extended weekends—which would allow us to experience the community as we never had before.

After that last idea, we all became much more positive and started fleshing out the ideas. The "disaster" turned into an "experience" that, by and large, we all enjoyed.

This Practice Helps Us Engage with Personal Challenges

Most of us have met people who display uncommon grace in the face of personal tragedy. Such people make us say to ourselves, "I hope I can be positive as that about life, should I ever have such a terrible experience."

(Bob) Less than a year ago, a friend of mine learned that he had inoperable liver cancer. He was 85 and still a strong skier—I know because I skied with him just after this.

At the beginning of the winter, when he was diagnosed with cancer, his doctors encouraged him to start chemotherapy right away. He hesitated, thinking it would likely prevent him from enjoying his skiing and possibly even mean he could not ski at all.

So he decided to leave the chemo until after ski season. "This could be my last year and I'm going to enjoy it!" he said.

This despite the fact that delaying the chemotherapy may have reduced his chances of recovery.

Peter had always been able to perceive the positives. I would wager that if I had asked him to find four positives in the diagnosis he received, he would have been able to do so. Here are some of the things he would have said:

- I have an opportunity to deliberately get in touch with a lot of people who mean something to me and say a proper goodbye.
- I have time to get my financial affairs in order so I know my wife won't have anything to worry about.
- This is an opportunity to become really engaged and focused on the present.

Peter died in June, following the ski season. The last thing he said to me was, "Hey, Bob, I'm 85. I've had a great run and I'm OK to move on."

The tributes to his positive frame of mind flowed richly at his memorial service.

Even in the most difficult, the most serious situation, you can muster more energy and deal with the situation more effectively if you perceive the positives instead of being overcome by your ARGUEing emotions. This energy will in turn be transferred to those supporting you through this difficult period. You allow the experience to become one of growth and opportunity, instead of one of fear and despair.

Downsides and Wishes

You do have to be careful that in striving to see the positive aspects of a situation you don't blind yourself to the issues that do indeed exist. Perceiving the positives does not preclude staying mindfully aware and thoughtfully authentic. What is important is to see the challenges in a positive context, so you approach issues with your energy flowing, not blocked. One way of doing this is to formulate the perceived drawbacks of a situation or idea as a wish, as Adam did in the example earlier in this chapter.

You'll usually find you're very aware of the downsides. The trick now is to frame them as *wishes* or *goals*. "I like this, this, this, and this about the idea—and I wish that we could address this aspect over here." Suddenly your energy now becomes focused on fixing what needs to be fixed.

> *(Bob)* I like the sound of flowing water. When we moved into our house just before the birth of our daughter, I built a pond and a stream fed by recirculating water from the pond. While it delivered the effect I was looking for, there was always a leak somewhere in the stream, and the water kept draining out of the pond. I spent hours—OK, days—every year trying to solve the problem.
>
> I could sense my wife getting somewhat frustrated over all the time I was spending on the failed repair. Then one day she said to me, "You know, I really like the idea of the running water and the pond. It's pretty there beside the deck, and the sound helps to mask the noise of the road traffic. It's also a demonstration of the creative things you can do yourself without having to spend the money on hiring others to do it, and I know you

enjoy working on it, even trying to fix the problem with the leaks. And I wish the leak problem could be fixed once and for all and get rid of the frustration you've had with it all these years."

Can you find the four positives in her response? They're there.

I found my response interesting. Instead of reacting defensively—considering my inability to fix the leak problem—I immediately started thinking about answers to her "wish."

We explored a number of options, and in the end turned to my nephew's partner, who was just starting a landscape design business. He was able to redesign and reconstruct the pond and stream, producing something that didn't leak, and at a "family discount." In return, knowing that it was "family," he got the opportunity to try out some different ideas and techniques to make more reliable steep streams, knowledge that he could transfer to other projects.

As we've seen, there are two steps you can take to get through a challenging situation:

- Push yourself to perceive the four positives.
- State the drawbacks you see in a wish format.

These two steps will positively influence your thoughts and feelings, change your own brain chemistry, and allow the energy to flow more easily. By perceiving the positives, you will keep yourself open to all that life may bring you.

Making Openness Work for You

The two of us apply the practices of openness in very different ways.

(Bob) For me, the mindset I choose to hold in the moment prepares my mental ground to be open—or not. By starting with the frame of mind that accepts the inevitable relevance of every idea, I avoid prematurely killing off a potentially useful idea. I have also found that my resulting demeanor encourages the energy flow of those around me.

While it's very similar to the practice of suspending judgment (chapter 11), my distinction is that the latter is a conscious action, while this practice is a more passive acceptance that allows ideas to germinate without my having to do anything.

When I feel myself closing down, and closing out new or different ideas, I will often turn to the practice of making fresh associations. This helps me return my thought patterns to being more open. And when my frame of mind is more open, I find myself more sincerely and enthusiastically identifying and stating the four positives.

(Julia) I start off by looking for what I like. In other words, perceiving the positives is my jumping-off point. I find that when I begin a dialogue with that notion, it's easier for me to entertain the idea that every idea is relevant—even if I don't yet know how that relevance will manifest itself. That means it's just a hop, skip, and a jump for me to move on to allowing and appreciating fresh associations.

The result is that my Thoughtful I is prepared to wait for an idea to eventually have relevance and to wait for solutions that will appear when least expected. I find it much easier to approach a situation assuming that my Thoughtful I will find something to like. And because I love the feeling that perceiving the fourth positive gives me, it's become a challenge instead of a chore to find it. Being open is so much better for my energy than being closed.

So how do you begin adopting these three practices to enhance your level of openness to ideas that are being presented to you, either by others or by your own mind?

Start by checking in with yourself every so often and asking the questions:

- Am I staying open to ideas?
- How do I know?

Then, if you're not satisfied with your answers, think about which of the three practices would be most useful to you in enhancing your openness.

UNDERSTANDING

The Thoughtful I and Understanding

The vowels of awareness, engagement, and openness, and the practices associated with each one, culminate powerfully in the vowel of understanding. In fact, the practices of understanding are the ultimate test of the other vowels and their practices. Being mindfully aware, staying engaged, and remaining open to new ideas put you into a frame of mind that allows you to fully develop your understanding of a situation.

The more you *understand*—not just *know about*—a situation, the better you can frame your response and the better you can take appropriate action. That's the premise of the Thoughtful I and understanding—how you can get to a point where you develop a more complete and comprehensive understanding.

First you must accept that the way you survive in this relative world is by making choices. Your life is not about your abilities. It's about your choices. And the more deeply you understand something, the more beneficial your choices are going to be to you in creating your own reality.

This section, on understanding, therefore lays out three practices:

- Acknowledge—and Suspend—Judgment
- Confirm Your Understanding
- Embrace the Power of the Both/And

11

Acknowledge—and Suspend—Judgment

The impulse to judge is in the very warp and woof of our natures and personal histories. And our judging can get us into all manner of difficulties. This chapter looks at the ways you have of judging—not just people but ideas as well—and at the consequences of these kinds of judgment.

Three Different Kinds of Judgment

In discussing this practice we refer to three different types of thought, each of which we call "judgment": perception, preference, and prejudice. It may be worth taking a few moments here to distinguish between these three.

Perception

Perception, or discernment, allows you to distinguish between things without preference, but with a base of reference. It is a distinction based on **observation**. You can look at two plants and think or say, "This plant appears green and vigorous, while that one appears brown and wilted." Of course, you have had to learn what "brown and wilted" and "green and vigorous" are to make these observations and distinctions.

An expression of innocent perception will normally have no material impact on the flow of energy in and of itself. At the same time, it will add to the base of shared knowledge.

Preference

Preference, which leads to choice, brings in the personal **biases** that you've built up over time. You look at the two plants and think or say, "I prefer the green plant—it's certainly healthier." Of course, "healthy" is tied only to what you have learned to think is pretty.

And this may lead you to the decision, "I will buy the green plant even though the wilted one has the color of flower I like better," which is a judgment that now moves you along a particular path—planting a garden with an initially green and vigorous plant. The basis of your choice is your preference for starting with what you consider a healthy plant.

A preference leading to a choice directs the flow of energy along a particular path so it becomes useful at some point. Prematurely expressed, this judgment limits the possible choices. Deferred, it misses the opportunity.

Prejudice

Prejudice is based on some deeper **thoughts** and personal **beliefs**. You look at the plants and think or say, "I can't believe the owner of this store would display dead plants on those shelves. It's clear he doesn't even know how to take care of greenery."

Prejudice is the most dangerous of the three classes of judgment, especially in its negative form, which tends to manifest itself as *con-demnation*. It's clear that a condemning thought will divert your internal flow of energy, and a condemnation expressed will have a negative impact on the energy exchange.

If you're like most people, you spend little time declaring your discernments and instead jump right to one or both of the other kinds of judgment. Many people evaluate and make choices automatically, without considering the options. And most make prejudicial judgments continually, whether they declare them openly or not. In most of what follows, therefore, we'll be referring to the second and third types of judgment, preference and prejudice.

In *suspending judgment*, the trick is for you to determine how any expression of judgment will affect the flow of personal creative energy, either within yourself or between you and others. By staying mindfully aware, you can learn to distinguish between all your different judgments. And you can determine how best to act, knowing whether suspending or holding onto that judgment will help or hinder the flow of energy.

Acknowledge Your Judgments

The first step in this practice is to be mindfully aware that you are making a judgment.

The second step is to acknowledge that your judgments are part of your humanity. After all, when our ancestors felt the threat of danger, they had to make a judgment—whether to fight or to flee. In The Energy Exchange, we want to be aware of, and acknowledge, a judgment before it has an impact on the situation.

You grow up learning to make judgments. When you take your first steps, you are making a series of judgments. When you turn your nose up at the squash and eagerly reach for the carrots, you are making a judgment. These judgments result in responses from your parents, siblings, and teachers, all of which influence the development of your repertoire of automatic behaviors. Making these judgments, whether they are helpful and good or not, becomes a matter of course and part of who you are.

Let's consider a child who is learning to walk. He finds himself up against a gate—one of those designed to prevent him from going down the stairs—and to his delight, the gate falls when he pushes on it. Now he can try the stairs. What he does not realize is that walking down the stairs is not the same as walking on a floor. He falls, starts to cry, and is rescued by his mother. She tells him that when he sees a gate, he should not go through it.

And from that point, every time the boy sees one, he decides to find a way around it. He has a judgment about gates. Eventually, he transfers this judgment to fences, too, and avoids climbing fences at all costs.

He may even become an expert at rock climbing and yet still stay away from fences. Logical? No. Rational? No. Limiting? Yes.

What if that fence was standing between the young man and something he really wanted? Couldn't his rock-climbing skill be applied to this challenge? Almost certainly. And yet, the memory of that gate and the fall down the stairs stays with him, blocking his energy and stopping him in his tracks. It prevents him from even exploring the option of climbing the fence.

If the young man were to acknowledge the judgment, he would have the opportunity to work around it. He may still end up deciding not to climb the fence, but if he acknowledges his judgment from the start, it will be easier for him to entertain other possibilities.

> *(Julia)* When we have this kind of natural reaction, and want to keep the energy flowing, the best thing to do is to acknowledge our humanity. It's important that we not scold ourselves for passing the judgment—that makes it all about me. If that happens, our own energy will be blocked and we'll be unable to find creative solutions.
>
> I remember when my husband and I first met and he invited me to go sailing with him. I had had a scary experience with a motorboat when I was about seven. From then on, I avoided boats with motors (I was fine in a canoe). I could feel my judgment filling my mind and body. I hesitated, and he asked me if I had ever been sailing. I told him that the only boat I had been on was a motorboat and it hadn't been a good experience.
>
> He didn't laugh at me (which I was afraid he would do). Instead, he said he thought I might like the silence of sailing. He also said he would bring another friend who knew how to crew, so I would be able to relax and "enjoy the ride."
>
> As I look back, I realize that he was acknowledging the validity of my judgment and also encouraging me to suspend it. I accepted his invitation.

Suspend Your Judgment

Acknowledging your judgment doesn't necessarily mean you're going to act on it. It simply means you are accepting its existence. When you have acknowledged it, the next step is to grab it, pull it aside, and hang it on a hook out of your range of vision. This way, you can allow the suspended judgment to stay available for inspection and to continue to be taken seriously.

(Bob) When Dorothy and I were first in the market for a house—our daughter's birth was seven months away—we set up the parameters for the purchase. I had a long-time personal friend, Andrew, in the residential renovation business, so we were looking for a building to gut and convert into something that reflected our unique requirements and tastes.

After waiting six weeks and not hearing anything from our real estate agent, we got the call: "Be at this address at 4 p.m. today. I'll arrange for Andrew to meet us there. This is a pre-showing; the house won't be listed until next week."

When Dorothy and I entered the house, we almost turned on our heels and left. The inside smelled of cat urine; the walls were grungy, the backyard was an unkempt tangle of weeds; and all the rooms were tiny and dark. It was really demanding to suspend our judgment about buying this place.

When Andrew arrived, the first thing he said was, "Bob, forget what's here. Let it disappear." And while he and I walked around the house redesigning it, Dorothy sat with the owner of the house and learned its history.

When Andrew and I were done, we all left. Dorothy couldn't get out of there fast enough. On reflection, it would have been more powerful to have walked her around the house talking about the possibilities so she could see its potential.

While it stretched our budget, we put in an offer that day, making it as easy as possible for the owner to say "yes." The next day we owned it, and the buzz on the street was that if it had been listed on the market, it would have sold for a much higher price.

Suspending our judgment gave us a home that we still take great pleasure in.

Suspending your judgments until you get all the data will inform whatever decisions you end up making. When you do make a final choice, it will have a better chance of succeeding because you've been open to all the possibilities.

At the same time, it helps if you can increase your use of the perception type of judgment. When you observe and absorb without preference, looking through the eyes of the artist who sees what's there with innocent perception, you give yourself the chance to build your knowledge of what you see in front of you before choosing your path.

Judgments Can Limit You ... and Others

Prejudicial judgments have a way of becoming assumptions and sparking the creation of stereotypes. As you become more and more mindfully aware, you will begin to see that these assumptions and stereotypes have the power to block your creative energy. You want to make sure you don't allow them to inform your decisions and limit your opportunities, and the opportunities of others.

(Julia) Let's say, for example, that I think short people can't play basketball. What I have done is limit my own opportunities to engage in a team sport, and, perhaps more importantly, I am limiting my son's possibilities. In fact, when it was time for team tryouts, and he told me he was going to try out for the

soccer and basketball teams, I said I thought he would have a better chance of getting on the soccer team.

Later that week, I told my mother he was trying out for both teams and that I thought he was too short to get on the basketball team. I was surprised to hear her say, "Julia, of course he can play basketball. I did, and I was only five feet tall at the time—the shortest person in my grade. I was a pretty decent scorer, too. I ran between the legs of the really tall players!"

Our son, as it turned out, did make both teams.

Judgments Can Lead to Emotional Hijacking

Often, you'll find yourself in a position where you're ascribing intent to someone's statement or action without any real basis other than your own rambling thoughts.

(Bob) Generally my wife considers herself a patient, understanding, and non-aggressive driver. That's especially true when it comes to parking. She will often park blocks from where she wants to go in order to avoid the dreaded *parallel parking* spot. When she sees someone having difficulty squeezing between two cars on a busy street, she silently cheers them on, admiring their courage for attempting this almost impossible procedure.

One day she was running several errands and had just five minutes to complete the last one before picking up our daughter at school. After she circled the area a few times, a spot became available ... between two other cars. She looked at her watch and decided she was going to have to bite the bullet and parallel park.

Just as she was about to try to slide into the spot, she noticed the person in the car behind the spot was on the way out. So, poised to park, she waited for her to leave. She waited and waited and waited. Time was running out and she was going to be late to pick up our daughter.

After a few minutes, believing that this person was not going to leave for a while, she parked. It took a few tries, but she managed. Not, however, without directing some nasty thoughts toward the person behind her.

Just as Dorothy was getting out of the car to pay the meter, the other woman popped out of her car and offered her her parking ticket. She had overpaid by more than an hour and was waiting to give it away. Instantly, my wife told me, that sheepish feeling that comes from having judged the thoughts and intents of others on a shaky foundation swept over her.

When you feel your judgment coming out in this kind of situation, it's time to go back to the thought that generated it and change it, allowing the judgment to disappear.

These kinds of judgments—formulating intent without proof—can happen just as easily with people you're close to. How often have you thought or said, when a close friend or spouse has started to say something, "I know what you're going to say," finding that something entirely different comes out? When you feel your judgment rising in your throat, you need to suspend the judgment and go back to listening.

Listening to Unlikely Sources

Any systemic judgments that you allow to exist—any prejudices and stereotypes that you hold onto—will limit your opportunities and those of others. You create the conditions for energy to be blocked, and so your judgments eventually become self-fulfilling prophecies.

> *(Bob)* When we formed our management-consulting firm in the early 1990s, one of the early things we wanted to create was a tagline we could print at the bottom of our letterhead.
>
> We brought several professionals together and invited a couple of administrative assistants along to "observe" and get a better sense of the firm. As we started our brainstorming exercise, trying out possible taglines, I had the sense that we were operating on an unwritten rule that only the professionals were to participate.
>
> We had generated a few rather uninspired statements, when one of the admin assistants blurted out a phrase that caught everyone off guard. I could sense by the looks on individuals' faces and the increased tension in the room that people were thinking, "Who does she think she is to toss out an idea?" After a few moments, however, everyone seemed to recognize that the statement was funny, highly creative, and slightly outrageous. In the end, it formed the basis of the tagline that we eventually selected.

The systemic nature of these judgments can be related to job position, nationality, education level, religion, income, or any number of categories. Often, you will not even be aware that you hold these prejudices. When you do become aware of them, once again, you need to revisit the thoughts and the underlying beliefs you are holding, and change them appropriately.

This Practice Increases Energy Flow and Ideas

When you acknowledge and suspend your own judgment, you enable your own energy to flow freely. It becomes contagious. Because you are open to others and their ideas, they feel more open to you and are more willing to share their ideas.

> *(Bob)* Remember the story I told earlier about our daughter talking about "the both-handed"? While my response *was* somewhat of a judgment, albeit a positive one, it certainly required me to suspend my judgment that a child is not really able to contribute to this material.
>
> In suspending my judgment, it encouraged Rome to generate even *more* ideas with the potential of having a substantial impact on how we communicate our models.

Acknowledging and suspending judgment allows for the free flow of energy and for the resulting free exchange of ideas. This is an essential element in accepting and supporting our mutuality.

> *(Julia)* When I'm facilitating a program for adult learners, I have a rule that no one is allowed to comment on or dismiss anyone's idea or question, regardless of how silly or weird it may seem. I ask that when they feel a judgment coming on, they first of all acknowledge it and accept their human condition. I then ask them to "reach down their own throat" and pull the judgment out, so they can suspend it on a hook—hang it out to dry, so to speak. That way, their judgment is still there and acknowledged, but it doesn't get in the way of the process of giving every idea the chance to be considered.

Once all the ideas are on the table, I say that we can revisit the suspended judgments as a group and take them into consideration as we make our decision. That way, the judgments neither influence the energy one way or the other nor block the flow of ideas.

Acknowledging and Suspending Judgment Improves Relationships

Acknowledging and suspending your judgments requires you to embrace the notion that the strongly held views that work for you may not be right in every situation. It can be particularly difficult to do this when it comes to people who are close to you.

(Bob) My brother and I have taken a very different approach to raising a family. Part of that comes from my having been 53 years old when our daughter was born. I continue to reflect that I was "too young to have kids" at the normal age. So by the time I started my parental experience, my brother's children were into their 30s.

As Dorothy and I made and enacted our decisions, my brother was often present, because he stayed with us when he came to Toronto from his home base in Halifax. In his wisdom, he never "shoulded" on us, electing rather to share his experience non-judgmentally, using statements like, "That's really interesting. You're certainly following a different path from the one Sue and I took."

Knowing my brother growing up—he's six years older than I am—I realized that this approach was not characteristic of him. Over the years he had learned to set aside his judgment and accept that others were on different paths.

And said with a warm smile, that avoidance of expressed judgment encouraged us to talk freely about other ways of doing things and to strengthen the bond between us.

The willingness to put aside an opinion or idea communicates that you're accepting that you may not be "right," or that at least you can't be sure you're right. This approach is more likely to encourage others to trust you over the long term.

Acknowledge and Suspend Positive Judgments, Too

It's easy to understand the usefulness of suspending our negative judgments, but what about positive ones?

What happens if we feel a judgment coming on? Why suspend it? How can it have a negative effect on the outcome?

(Bob) I have a long-time colleague who's a real techie. He researches new technologies thoroughly, makes a few mistakes in the process, and ends up making some wise decisions with respect to the products he buys. I have high respect for his knowledge, both for the technology itself and for how best to use it.

Recently he showed me an electronic notepad that he used for taking interview notes. He described the technology and how he used it with great enthusiasm. I got so excited that I went out and bought one myself.

After learning how to use it, I finally came to the conclusion that for my kind of interviewing, the product was not very helpful.

There went $200 down the drain.

Because you view someone as a good friend, or knowledgeable, or simply someone you like, you can sometimes automatically accept their suggestions as sound. Judging their ideas this way cuts you off from exploring other suggestions. They may be right, yet assuming too quickly that they are right could mean making a choice that's wrong for you. You'd be better off to accept their idea and suspend your judgment of it, good or bad, until you've explored all your options.

It can actually be just as dangerous to reveal a positive judgment as a negative one, especially in collaborative situations. In a brainstorming session, if someone voices an idea and the boss says, "That's great!", the boss is potentially cutting off the flow of other ideas. The group may start pursuing that idea to the exclusion of all others, missing out on some brilliant suggestions in the process.

Acknowledging and Suspending Judgment Can't Hurt You

This practice is a great way to protect yourself and others from the consequences of blocked energy. Still, it's useful to ask whether acknowledging and suspending your judgment can hurt you.

The answer is simple. It can't, unless it's a matter of life or death. If a situation is developing that you believe poses real danger to yourself or others, that's no time to be hanging your judgment out to dry. This kind of situation, thankfully, tends to be rare. In most cases, leaving yourself open to the ideas of others will be helpful. Your energy will flow more easily, as will the energy of those around you.

And yet, if using your judgment is part of making decisions, how do you acknowledge and suspend it in a way that assures you of the best result?

In the next two chapters, we introduce two practices—confirming our understanding and embracing the power of the both/and—that will help you do exactly that.

12

Confirm Your Understanding

When you have a good, shared understanding with people, everything else falls into place and there's little opportunity to get hijacked. Your own energy flows because you have a concrete understanding from which to move forward. The other person's energy flows because they feel understood and validated. Shared understanding lets you build ideas and relationships that are mutually appealing.

Confirming your understanding is a practice that goes hand in hand with acknowledging and suspending your judgment. After you have acknowledged your own judgment and set it aside, you are in a better position—a neutral position—to confirm your understanding of what the other person has said. This practice is hugely beneficial. When you express yourself and hear your thoughts being relayed back to you in a positive way, you feel good. You have been understood. You feel accepted and buoyant. And the energy flows. Without this practice, communication can be a very negative experience in which you feel ignored or misunderstood.

When young children begin to speak, their parents often repeat what they think the child has said. This does more than allow the child to hear how the word is supposed to be pronounced. It also lets the child *feel heard*. If the parent has not understood what the child has said, the child is likely to repeat it until the parent does understand. If the parent takes too long, the child may begin to cry. When the parent finally does understand, the child stops crying and starts smiling and the parent is relieved. Another step has been taken in language development, and, more importantly, in the parent–child relationship.

At some point, the parents understand what their child is saying, even if others don't. The parents make sure to translate what the child is saying so other people can understand and the child once again hears the correct pronunciation. The child does not feel the anger and frustration of not being heard and understood. The child's energy continues to flow.

Odd, isn't it, that we abandon the practice of making sure that we—and others—understand what a person is saying just because they speak clearly? How much more could we accomplish if we made sure we really did understand what other people were saying, or meant to say?

Grown-ups Need to Be Heard, Too

We know from dealing with children that *no* attention is even worse than *negative* attention. Not being paid any attention is often the cause of what we call "bad behavior."

What's fascinating is that the need to be given attention does not go away when we "grow up." We all still need to feel valued and respected. Therefore it's important to acknowledge other people's words, ideas, and opinions, even if we don't necessarily agree with them.

> *(Bob)* Confirming your understanding actually starts with the acknowledgment that you have heard someone. In group sessions I am facilitating, I will often ask someone to "hold that thought" so I can come back to it and confirm that I have understood it. As long as the individual knows I mean what I say and I will come back to it, the energy flow does not become blocked.

If you don't at least acknowledge a contribution, the individual is likely to feel ignored and will either disengage from the situation or become disruptive.

How Does It Work?

What do we mean by *confirm your understanding*? It's as simple as taking these three steps:

- First, let the other person know you are going to paraphrase what was said. Here's how that might sound: "Let me see if I understand your thought the way you meant it."
- Second, play back the thought in your own words, not just parrotting what the other person said.
- Third, ask the other person, "Did I get that right?"

> *(Julia)* When my mother was dying of cancer, it was really important for me to understand what the doctors were saying. My mother couldn't hear very well and was unfamiliar with the

doctors' jargon, so she mostly tuned out of the conversations we had with them.

It was a time of huge emotional stress, as you can imagine, and I am sure my mother was dealing with it the only way she could. Her response made it even more important for me to understand what the doctors were saying so that I could translate it for her—after all, isn't that what a patient advocate does?

I remember one particular instance when I got to go around the cycle of confirming my understanding at least twice before I actually "got it right." Here's what happened.

The doctor said: "We think it's ovarian cancer but we're not sure. More than 80% of the ovarian cancer we see is in women under 40. Assuming that it is ovarian cancer, it's an unusual type. We hardly ever see your mother's symptoms in women over 80. And it's also more aggressive than it is in 80% of the incidents of ovarian cancer we see in women over 80. Having said that, there is a chance that it is not ovarian. If it isn't, we don't know what it is. So we are going to treat it as if it is ovarian cancer, using a chemotherapy most frequently used on younger women. If it isn't ovarian cancer, we'll know when we have finished the chemo because we won't get the results we expect."

I almost laughed—I don't think my clients would let me get away with that kind of talk. I told the doctor I was going to paraphrase what I had heard him say.

"So you think that my mother more than likely has aggressive ovarian cancer, and you can't be sure," I said. "The treatment you're recommending should work if it is ovarian cancer, so you'll be in a better position to know more once the chemo is finished. There's not much else you can do, given the situation, and you are advising my mother to take the treatment."

The doctor said, "Yes, that's right. And I want to assure you that the chemo we are recommending will certainly reduce the mass that is causing your mother the most pain and preventing her from accepting nourishment."

I confirmed my understanding once again, and turned to my mother. "Mom, the doctors are recommending a treatment that will ease the pain the tumor is causing and help you start eating again. It's probably going to make you feel horrible for a while, and then you will feel better."

So it's as simple as saying, "Here's my understanding of what you just said. Did I get that right?" In our experience, if you've been engaged and actively listening, what you play back to the other individual will be on target most of the time. Others who are participating in the dialogue can become more engaged as a result of this practice, since many of them may have been reluctant to admit that they "just didn't get it." That's how this practice contributes to supporting mutuality, as well as developing real understanding.

Then it's the other person's turn. They listen to what you've just played back and let you know what you've got right and what you've missed. "OK. You got *this* part right. That's about 60% of it. Here's the 40% I think you missed." Or, "That's right. What I did not mention the first time is that…"—and then you have another opportunity to confirm what you just heard.

(Julia) Then something really interesting happened. After my second run at confirming my understanding, the doctor spoke

again. This time he spoke directly to my mother.

"Mrs. Gluck," he said, "you know we don't know everything. Your tests tell us some of what we need to know. We can create a chemo cocktail that can relieve your pain. The chemo won't be pleasant, but we think it's better for you in the long run. We may just be able to get you another year, maybe two, if we do that."

When—picking up on what I had done—the doctor used this simple language, my mother responded. It was as if she suddenly felt she was a person again and not a disease.

"So I won't like it," she said, with her characteristic shoulder shrug. " I've done lots of things I didn't like. Why not this one?"

"Good for you, Mrs. Gluck. That kind of positive energy will really help you get through this more easily," the doctor said.

When you attempt to confirm your understanding, you support the continued flow of energy and dialogue, giving the person being listened to a chance to make themselves clear without being put on the defensive. It also gives others a chance to confirm whether or not they understood what was said, encouraging the expansion of the dialogue. Once you have confirmed your understanding, it's much easier to disagree with them, because it's clear you're disagreeing with their idea and not with them as people.

Improving the Quality of the Dialogue and the Result

When you use this practice, you can improve the efficiency and effectiveness of your communication. When you're discussing a complex subject, you can separate the ideas for which you have a shared understanding from the ones for which you do not. By concentrating your efforts on the ideas that need clarification, you move the conversation forward, maintaining the kind of energy flow that supports a better result. This is easier when you combine the practice of confirming your understanding with the practice of perceiving the positives.

> *(Bob)* Earlier in the book, I talked about my recent experience working with a website designer who had some ideas I really liked. Given my experience with technical people, I made sure I confirmed my understanding of each idea as he gave them to me. It was when we got to some of the ideas I didn't necessarily like that this practice became even more useful.
>
> I realized that, having confirmed my understanding of the ideas that I did like, I had established a pattern with the designer. So he wasn't defensive when I confirmed that I understood one of his ideas and proceeded to tell him what I liked about it (four positives) and the one thing I wished could be handled differently. He listened to what I had to say and then— to my surprise and delight—asked if he could make sure he understood what I objected to.
>
> As he did so, it became obvious that there were some other pieces of information that he had left out (having made some judgments about how technical I was—or wasn't). He explained his idea some more, and while doing so, changed his mind about one thing, and, wouldn't you know it, we solved the problem.
>
> We continued to discuss the project in this fashion. When the designer left, he was in a position to write a proposal that was simply a confirmation of everything we had talked about in our meeting. Talk about a productive meeting!

Enabling the Energy to Flow Without Forcing It

Confirming your understanding lets people know that you value them and their opinions, even if you do not share those opinions. By making sure that you have understood another person, you strengthen your relationship with them and increase the possibility of getting better results.

Of course, you don't use this practice in order to impose your ideas on others. It's not meant to soften people up before you disagree with them. It's meant to validate the other person and prepare the ground for creative dialogue. This practice enables the flow of energy that comes when people feel valued—if not necessarily agreed with. The Energy Exchange practices are focused on "pull" rather than "push"—using a magnetic kind of energy. You can change the direction of the dialogue and the result without eliciting any ARGUE emotions, and instead gain the true consensus that comes from engagement and supportive mutuality.

(*Julia*) A friend asked me to help her plan a surprise 50th birthday party for her husband. I knew that Ian didn't like big crowds so I assumed the party was going to be a small one. When Diane said Ian didn't like surprises or birthday parties, and had an aversion to large crowds, my Thoughtful I could feel a judgment coming on. I acknowledged it, suspended it, and decided to try some confirming paraphrasing before I suggested that Diane was taking a big risk with this idea.

"So you want to have a surprise birthday party with about 60 people for your husband who does not like surprises, ignores his birthday every year, and would prefer to have dinner with one other couple, not two. Did I get that right?"

Diane laughed ruefully. She said she knew it probably was not a good idea, but she wanted to make Ian feel really special, and a big party was the only way she could think of to have all their friends and family participate in the celebration.

"So you have two things you want to do. One is to make sure he feels special, and the second one is to engage all your friends and family in recognizing this big birthday. And a party would certainly be a way to do that, except Ian doesn't like surprises or crowds."

Diane's energy was clearly getting blocked, so I quickly moved into finding four positives. "I really like that you want to make Ian feel special, and I also like the idea of getting family and friends involved. I like the idea of surprising him because otherwise he wouldn't let you do this, and I also like that you want to keep the party simple because that's the kind of guy Ian is."

Diane was tuned in. It was time for me to state my wish. "What I wish is that we could find a way to ease Ian into the discovery of his birthday celebration and have everyone involved, just not at the same time."

Diane perked up. "Tell me more about what you mean," she said. "How could we do that?"

I told her I wasn't sure and that I thought we would have to be really creative. Diane, who is an artist, ran for her easel and shouted to me from her studio, "I bet we can come up with some brilliant ideas. Let's get going!"

The result was a series of events during the week of Ian's birthday at his favorite places in the city. At each event, a small group of people gathered to help with the celebration, and Ian was able to spend some time with everyone who participated. Everyone agreed it was a great way to celebrate the big birthday.

13

Embrace the Power of the Both/And

It's in our nature to see ourselves as limited by choices. We tend to get caught up in the power of words like *but, either,* and *or*. We allow ourselves to be bound by the illusion of mutual exclusivity.

As you're going to see in this final chapter, it's amazing what happens when you allow yourself to move past *either/or* and embrace the power of the *both/and*.

> *(Julia)* We're so used to thinking in terms of one or the other. "You can do this or you can do that." "You can have long-term return on your investment, or you can have short-term return on your investment. You can't have both." And that's not necessarily true! I probably *can* find a way to get both short-term and longer-term return on my investment. That's where real performance is.

The words themselves have power. Many people, staying mindfully aware, will notice how their energy changes when they hear the words *either/or*. They may have a physical response, a feeling of being hemmed in, as if there's a fence around them, preventing them from using their energy to reach the other option. It may be an ARGUE response, a feeling of anger or resentment, a reminder of childhood when they did not yet understand the notion of limits.

This blocked energy stands in contrast to how people feel when they hear the words *both/and*. Think about this in your own experience. Notice how your breathing changes when you think of possibilities instead of limits? When you move away the *either/or*, you liberate your creative energy so that you can begin to imagine how seeming opposites could work together to produce a greater whole.

From the Tyranny of Either/Or to the Liberation of Both/And

Very often these opposites aren't opposites at all—it's just the way you set them up in your mind. Perhaps, in your experience to date, those two things have never existed together. Perhaps you set up these limits because you're afraid of some outcome or because of other limitations to your energy.

> *(Bob)* One morning when she was three my daughter came up to me and said, "Daddy, can I have something unhealthy to eat?" (For those not in the know, "unhealthy" means "loaded with sugar.")
>
> I said, "OK, would you like a popsicle *or* an ice cream bar?" She responded with, "I would like a popsicle … *and* an ice cream bar."
>
> I had a choice of where I could go. I could say, "No, you don't

have that option. It's either a popsicle or an ice cream bar." But I didn't want to be that rigid—my priority was not to say no, or to impose a rule, but simply to ensure that her consumption of sugar was limited. And we worked together to come up with a plan.

She decided to have half the popsicle and half the ice cream bar, and wrap the other halves up and put them back in the freezer for tomorrow. And there it was! She met her needs of the *both/and* and I met my desire for her to have less sugar.

The very next day she went back and did the same, except she had the ice cream bar first and then the popsicle.

Most often, when you have an *either/or*, it's because you have implicit assumptions about what you'll be able to do or to have. "I can't do them both," you tell yourself, "because I don't have enough time"—or money, or energy.

The solution, in these cases, is to get it all on the table and really look at your options. Is there a way to imagine having both? What if you found a way to be more efficient, to expend fewer resources and still have it all? What if you alter your thinking about the timeline? Figure out a strategy that turns the either/or into a both/and.

(Julia) It's a challenge for a lot of parents I know to accommodate and support their kids' multiple interests and ambitions. My neighbor's son, for example, loves skiing and hockey, and is good at both. It was that very skill that almost became a problem for the entire family.

To my friend, skiing meant spending his weekends driving his son to the various ski facilities where the races are held, and skating meant getting up at 4:30 on weekday mornings to take him to the rink. He wanted to support his son and the idea of taking on both of these obligations was overwhelming to him. He found himself wanting to tell his son that he had to choose one or the other.

To his credit, he wondered if it really had to be like that. Why should it only be one or the other? So he put all the information out on the table. He told his son, "Listen, I really admire your desire to get into both sports—they're equally challenging and exciting, and they'll teach you different things. At the same time, I really don't want to drive you all around the province on the weekends and still get up at 4 a.m. during the week. I am not that strong. I have work to do. However, I *am* willing to support you in one of them. So the challenge is how to get the other one covered, and which one it'll be."

Once he'd made his feelings clear, they could proceed to the real issue—the question of how to do both skiing and hockey. His son came up with a plan to bypass the *either/or*.

"Well, Dad," he said, "if I can arrange with Sally's mom to take me to hockey every morning and Jim's dad to take me skiing, would that be OK?"

My friend was thrilled, and why not? He got to get up at a normal hour every day and have his weekends—and still know that his son was getting what he needed.

"That would be great, David," he said, and then was touched by his son's next statement.

"By the way, Dad, whenever I have a tournament, I really hope you'll be able to come and watch."

What are the possibilities? What are the options? What are the aspects of each idea that you really like? What are the drawbacks?

How could you bring them together so that you get the advantages of both and minimize or eliminate any negatives associated with them?

The Both/And Holds More Power Than the Either/Or

You will often find yourself wrestling with two thoughts that *appear* to be in conflict. If you let the conflict block your energy, you will have to make a choice. If you take a both/and stance, you open up the possibilities.

> *(Bob)* This kind of thing happens frequently with sports teams who are having performance issues. There was an example of this recently, when the 2006 NHL hockey trade deadline was coming up. The Toronto Maple Leafs had had a weak season. They were not likely to make it to the playoffs. A team like that may seem to be in an either/or situation.
>
> "We'll go into the trade negotiations with a strategy of building for the future," officials of the team were saying on TV and radio. "We've had a tough year, so we'll trade some players and get some talent that we can develop for next year and the year after that."
>
> The situation was formulated as we *either* go for short-term help—in other words, older, more experienced players with a couple more years in them—in order to have a chance to make the playoffs, *or* we get some promising young players and start to build a team that will have a chance to make the playoffs next year or the year after.
>
> How can something like this be turned into a both/and? Is there any way to get some players who can help get the team to

the playoffs *and* help them rebuild toward next year? Could they trade for some young players to help them next year, who will also have the skills and energy now to help them get to the playoffs this year?

The goal for the general manager may be to choose players who improve the team's chances because of how adaptable they are—players who *both* give them a strong chance of actually making the playoffs this year *and* can play a part in rebuilding the team in the seasons to come.

Increasing the Energy Flow and Supporting Experimentation

When you're a slave to the either/or, you block the energy flow and miss out on a lot of creative ideas. When you embrace the both/and, you have the power of the energy flow working for you. You have the power to imagine all of your options.

And you don't have to do everything all at once. When you've considered a situation fully, you may decide to do one, or the other, or harmonize the two in some novel way. When you finally make your choice, you do so in a context very different from the one you found yourself in at the start—you do so in a context filled with opportunities instead of limitations.

When you combine the practice of embracing the power of the both/and with others from The Energy Exchange, such as perceiving the positives, you'll find that even more energy is liberated, that people are working together more effectively toward a common goal, and that, in general, there is more awareness, engagement, and openness in the air, in addition to a greater understanding of your opportunities.

(Bob) Let's go back to the one about the popsicle and the ice cream bar for a moment. Sometimes we may find that we end up returning to our original choices, and that will be because of a reasoned selection process, not because of constraints to our thinking.

For example, having entertained the notion of splitting the ice cream bar and popsicle in half, Rome may find herself saying, "You know what, Dad? I'm going to have my whole ice cream bar today and have the popsicle tomorrow, rather than do the half and half thing. It was an interesting idea and I think it's better to have one today and one tomorrow—that way each of them will taste fresher. So I'm going to really enjoy the ice cream bar today, and I'll have the popsicle tomorrow."

This is still both/and, it's just separated by 24 hours. What's more, it obviates the necessity to even refer to the issue of sugar intake and helps the child practice some restraint by deferring part of her pleasure until the next day. It gives the child a sense of control over what she does, instead of having to "obey" her father. Doesn't this sound a whole lot easier than having an argument about food rules?

By embracing the power of the both/and, you allow yourself and those around you to choose freely from as many options as you can think of. You don't let your judgments limit your energy. When you succumb to either/or, you allow judgments to block your energy and cut yourself off from the creative exploration of ideas.

The mere act of suspending judgment, setting aside the apparent either/or choice for the moment, and exploring the situation to see what the possibilities are, will free your energy and creativity. Instead of feeling stuck in an either/or choice, you may find other avenues to explore with a lot more energy and passion. That willingness to experiment fosters more mindful awareness, gets you and others engaged, and keeps everyone open to ideas whose relevance may not yet be apparent.

> *(Julia)* I think that embracing the power of the both/and allows you to have a mindset that is ready for anything. I think it's worthwhile incorporating into any discussion I'm having—and I often substitute "and" for "but." It makes the conversation easier to have, keeps the energy flowing, and generally makes life a little easier to live.
>
> Since I have been doing this at home, I have found it easier to keep my shoulders away from my ears, easier to get others to listen to what I have to say, and easier to reach agreements that satisfy everyone in the house. I can feel the exchange of energy happening—that's the power of the both/and.

All of these things come together when you open your mind to allow the both/and to exist. So many of us tend to limit ourselves by saying, "We can't have it all."

Here's a better approach. You *can* have it all. So start dreaming about having it all.

Making Understanding Work for You

The way you apply the three practices of understanding will be unique to you and your grasp of all the other practices.

(Julia) With this vowel, I start with the middle practice. Confirming my understanding is the best way I know to convey to someone else that my energy is focused on them. I find when I am intent on making sure that I have understood someone, I have to acknowledge and suspend any judgment that I might have had, good or bad. By the time I have managed to rephrase what the other person has said—and by the way, I have often enough been corrected in doing so—it's much easier to embrace the power of the both/and.

So, understanding for me begins with the Thoughtful I being mindfully aware of where my energy is focused. It continues with my being fully engaged in the moment of dialogue and being open to whatever creative product results from the energy exchange taking place.

And when that happens, I feel I have really understood what "understanding" really means.

(Bob) The "U" is appropriately placed, to my mind, because it is the culmination of the other vowels. I know I can reach a full level of understanding when, through my Thoughtful I, I have stayed aware, engaged, and open.

I use the first two practices in tandem—suspending my judgment and confirming my understanding of what another person is saying. Do I "get it" all the time? No. And it certainly works a lot better than when I don't use the practices.

I also find that I can reinvigorate my energy flow when I hear two ideas that are in direct conflict, by imagining a situation where both ideas exist simultaneously. While I haven't always been able to make this state a reality, it has always led me to a better solution than the either/or condition.

For me, that "understanding" is liberating and energizing.

So how do you begin adopting these three practices to enhance your willingness and effort to seek understanding about what's going on around you?

Start by checking in with yourself every so often and asking the questions:

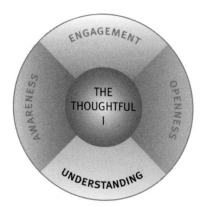

- Am I constantly seeking to understand?
- Am I confirming my understanding?
- How do I know?

Then, if you're not satisfied with the answers, think about which of the three practices would be most useful to you in enhancing your capability to seek and gain understanding

Conclusion:
And Always Why

The simple answer to "why" is "to allow healing energy to flow freely in and around your self and all your relationships."

Consistently using the practices embodied in *The Vowels of Personal Power* removes the plaque that has been building up in your creative energy channels since you were an infant.

Remember that you were born with these talents. Using the Thoughtful I, you reconnect with them and connect them to each other.

At the same time, adopting these practices is like raising children or teenagers. You'll make lots of mistakes as you figure out what's going on and what you're supposed to be doing. In the end, the practices will create a way of being, a way of looking at the world and your interaction with it, making the world a better place for you and others, a little bit at a time.

(Bob) When my department was putting together a management-training program in the 1980s, one of the concepts we

were exploring was the "power" of the manager. An important moment of enlightenment came when one of my colleagues said, "In the French language, there are two words for power—*puissance* and *pouvoir*. The first one means 'power over' and the second means 'power through.' In my experience, the manager who uses the second approach has a more lasting effect."

We heard a great story that fleshes out this message, and our book, rather well.

As a young woman was wrestling with a horse trying to get it under control, a wizened elderly trainer motioned her over.

"How much do you weigh, little lady?" he asked.

Overcoming her sense of affront, she told him.

"And how much does that horse of yours weigh?" he asked.

She guessed 1,500 pounds.

"So what makes you think that 130 pounds can control 1,500? If you're going to make any headway, you've got to become one with the horse. You must command the horse; you'll never control him."

And so it is with the vowels. You are much more effective when you use the practices to become one with your world. Yes, it's possible to use them to control others and get them to do what you want them to do, imposing your own distinct view of the world on those around you. Do this, however, and your gains will be fleeting and impermanent.

Alternatively, you can trust the process and integrate yourself with your world, ultimately gaining command of your own destiny. This is also what we mean by the "integrity" of the Thoughtful I.

Whether you acknowledge it or not, you are a spiritual being having a physical, mental, and emotional experience on this planet. You already know what you need to do to live in peace and harmony with all life in this world. And you're here to make a difference.

That "little better off" could be centered on one's family, community, or profession.

What do the vowels have to do with all this?

By keeping your Thoughtful I activated, staying aware, getting and staying engaged both in the moment and in who you want to become, being open to ideas that test your preferences and beliefs, and consistently seeking to understand, you remain a vital energy, making a difference in your world and having a blast in the process.

And to quote a character who made a difference: "God bless us, every one."

Bibliography

Berne, Eric. *Games People Play.* New York: Ballantine Books, 1973.

Bernstein, Albert J. *How to Deal with Emotionally Explosive People.* New York: McGraw-Hill, 2003.

Bohm, David. *On Dialogue.* London: Routledge, 1996.

Braden, Gregg. *Awakening to Zero Point: The Collective Initiation.* Bellevue, WA: Radio Bookstore Press, 1993, 1997.

Carey, Ken. *The Third Millennium: Living in the Posthistoric World.* San Francisco: HarperCollins, 1991.

Chopra, Deepak. *The Seven Spiritual Laws of Success: A Practical Guide to the Fulfillment of Your Dreams.* San Rafael, CA: Amber-Allen Publishing and New World Library, 1994.

Collins, Jim. *Good to Great: Why Some Companies Make the Leap ... and Others Don't.* New York: HarperCollins, 2001.

Covey, Stephen R. *The Seven Habits of Highly Effective People: Powerful Lessons in Personal Change.* New York: Simon & Shuster, 1989.

De Saint-Exupéry, Antoine. *A Guide for Grown-ups: Essential Wisdom from the Collected Works*. Orlando, FL: Harcourt, 2002.

Fisher, Roger, William Ury. *Getting to Yes: Negotiating Agreement Without Giving In*. Boston: Houghton Mifflin, 1981.

Gladwell, Malcolm. *The Tipping Point: How Little Things Can Make a Big Difference*. Boston: Little, Brown, 2000.

Gleick, James. *Chaos: The Making of a New Science*. New York: Penguin, 1989.

Green, Glenda. *Love Without End: Jesus Speaks*. Fort Worth, TX: Spiritis Publishing, 1999, 2002.

Hagan Stacie, Charlie Palmgren. *The Chicken Conspiracy: Breaking the Cycle of Personal Stress and Organizatinal Mediocrity*. Baltimore: Recovery Communications, 1998.

Hawkins, David R. *Power vs. Force: The Hidden Determinants of Human Behavior*. West Sedona, AZ: Veritas Publishing, 1995, 2004.

Hunt, Valerie V. *Infinite Mind: Science of the Human Consciousness*. Malibu, CA: Malibu Publishing, 1989, 1996.

Johnson, Spencer, M.D. *Who Moved My Cheese?* New York: G.P. Putnam's, 1999.

Levoy, Gregg. *Callings: Finding and Following an Authentic Life*. New York: Random House, 1997.

Losier, Michael J. *Law of Attraction: The Science of Attracting More of What You Want and Less of What You Don't*. Victoria, BC, 2003.

Miller, Anne. *Metaphorically Selling: How to Use the Magic of Metaphors to Sell, Persuade, and Explain Anything to Anyone*. New York: Chiron Associates, 2004.

Olmsted, Michael S. *The Small Group*. New York: Random House, 1959.

Patterson, Kerry, Joseph Grenny, Ron McMillan, Al Switzler. *Crucial Conversations: Tools for Talking When Stakes Are High*. New York: McGraw-Hill, 2002.

Prince, George M. *The Practice of Creativity*. New York: Macmillan, 1970.

Rodegast, Pat, Judith Stanton. *Emmanuel's Book* (vols. I, II, and III). New York: Bantam Books, 1985, 1989, 1994.

Scott, Susan. *Fierce Conversations: Achieving Success at Work and in Life, One Conversation at a Time*. New York: Berkley Publishing Group, 2002.

Shekerjian, Denise. *Uncommon Genius: How Great Ideas Are Born*. New York: Penguin Books, 1990.

Simmons, Susan LePage. *What If? 310 Bite-Size Brain Snacks to Spark Your Creative Spirit*. Toronto: Simmons Group, 1994.

Smith, Hyrum W. *The Ten Natural Laws of Successful Time and Life Management: Proven Strategies for Increased Productivity and Inner Peace*. New York: Warner Books, 1994.

Tolle, Eckhart. *The Power of Now: A Guide to Spiritual Enlightenment*. Vancouver: Namaste Publishing, 1997.

Von Oech, Roger. *Expect the Unexpected or You Won't Find It: A Creativity Tool Based on the Ancient Wisdom of Heraclitus*. San Francisco: Berrett-Koehler, 2002.

Wilkins, Rob. *Taking the Child's Way Home*. Grand Rapids, MI: Zondervan, 1995.

Young, James Webb. *A Technique for Producing Ideas*. New York: McGraw-Hill, 2003.

Zander, Rosamund Stone, Benjamin Zander. *The Art of Possibility: Transforming Professional and Personal Life*. Boston: Harvard Business School Press, 2000.